THE TRUTH ABOUT

PAYING FEWER TAXES

S. Kay Bell

First Printing January 2009

ISBN-10   0-13-715386-4
ISBN-13   978-0-13-715386-2

Pearson Education LTD.
Pearson Education Australia PTY, Limited.
Pearson Education Singapore, Pte. Ltd.
Pearson Education North Asia, Ltd.
Pearson Education Canada, Ltd.
Pearson Educatión de Mexico, S.A. de C.V.
Pearson Education—Japan
Pearson Education Malaysia, Pte. Ltd.

Library of Congress Cataloging-in-Publication Data

Bell, S. Kay, 1956-
   The truth about paying fewer taxes / S. Kay Bell.
      p. cm.

   ISBN 0-13-715386-4 (pbk.   alk. paper) 1. Income tax--United States. I. Title.
   HJ4652.B36 2009
   343.7305'2--dc22
                        2008039901

Vice President, Publisher
Tim Moore

Associate Publisher and Director of Marketing
Amy Neidlinger

Executive Editor
Jim Boyd

Editorial Assistant
Myesha Graham

Development Editor
Russ Hall

Operations Manager
Gina Kanouse

Digital Marketing Manager
Julie Phifer

Publicity Manager
Laura Czaja

Assistant Marketing Manager
Megan Colvin

Cover and Interior Designs
Stuart Jackman, Dorling Kindersley

Design Manager
Sandra Schroeder

Managing Editor
Kristy Hart

Project Editor
Jovana San Nicolas-Shirley

Copy Editor
Water Crest Publishing, Inc.

Proofreader
San Dee Phillips

Senior Compositor
Gloria Schurick

Manufacturing Buyer
Dan Uhrig

This book is dedicated to my husband,
who hates taxes but who lovingly tolerates,
and sometimes even encourages, my tax obsession.

Introduction

Every year, more than 130 million Americans face one of life's most dreaded tasks: filing their federal income tax returns.

But the truth about taxes is that they are much more than a once-a-year ordeal. They are constant, albeit uninvited, companions in our lives.

Taxes and their real-life effects began on day one, when our delivery room cries signaled a new tax break for our parents. And taxes continue to share our lives as we get and change jobs, start our families, increase our assets, and make plans to help ensure the financial future of our heirs.

At every one of these major milestones, the tax opportunities and pitfalls are myriad and their financial implications are huge. Yet most of us try to deal with taxes as little as possible. Typically, we put off the intimidating and maddening task of tax filing until the last minute. Worse, we put off tax planning completely. The trouble with this all-too-prevalent attitude is that the cost is often literal and large.

But it doesn't have to be that way.

Although our tax laws require that you pay what you owe, they don't demand that you overpay. In fact, the Internal Revenue Code is full of ways to trim your eventual IRS bill. This book will help you realize just how these laws can be used to your maximum tax-saving advantage.

Over the years, I've dealt with taxes from a variety of perspectives. As a taxpayer, I encounter the same frustrations you do each filing season. As a Congressional staff member, I witnessed firsthand the creation of some of these aggravating tax laws. And as a writer who has focused on tax issues on an almost-daily basis for the last decade, I've learned that most of us simply want an understandable way to meet our tax responsibilities.

That's where *The Truth About Paying Fewer Taxes* comes in. This is not a line-by-line, how-to-file-your-return book. Neither is it an all-inclusive look at the Internal Revenue Code. That's a nearly impossible task, because our tax laws now fill around 68,000 pages.

Rather, it's an overview of key tax laws that affect the lives of most of us and the truth about how to make them work in our favor. When you finish reading, you'll be ready to tackle your taxes or discuss them more confidently with your tax adviser, with a solid grasp of what to expect, avoid, and make the most of.

The core of the book is organized around the major life stages that offer many tax obstacles and opportunities: how taxes and tax breaks apply to your family, your career, your home, your investments, and your eventual retirement.

Sandwiching those high points in your life are some universal tax considerations, starting with a look at general filing issues, tips, and ways to reduce your taxable income, and closing with some compliance concerns and a discussion of special tax circumstances.

Regardless of where you are in your personal and tax-paying life, you'll find a chapter or two or more that affects you. Perhaps only one section applies to you now; perhaps you can make use of several. Each section, indeed each of the 52 chapters, is self-contained, so read this book at your own pace, picking and choosing chapters as your circumstances demand.

But don't be afraid to check out those areas in which taxes aren't yet a concern to you. Eventually, they probably will be. And by taking a sneak peek, you'll be prepared when you do embark on a new phase of your life and its tax consequences.

More importantly, with your newfound grasp on the many tax implications at each stage of your life, you'll be able to maximize your tax savings or at least minimize your tax burden.

TRUTH

Not everyone has to file

Taxes are truly one of the most egalitarian of institutions. Young and old, rich and poor, living in the United States or abroad, most Americans must deal with paying what has been described as the price of a civilized society.

But the U.S. tax code's reach, while long, is not absolute. In fact, for some folks, April 15 is just another day because they don't have to worry about filing a return.

How do these lucky individuals get off the tax hook? They don't meet the filing requirements. But arriving at that fortunate tax place requires assessment of three different factors.

Generally, whether the IRS requires a 1040 from you is determined by the following:

1. Your income
2. Your filing status
3. Your age

Income—The primary consideration is how much you make. It is, after all, called an income tax. And after you make a certain amount

Gross income is all the compensation you receive. It can be as money, goods, property, and even services. Income from sources outside the United States also must be counted when considering whether you make enough to require a 1040 submission.

Self-employment income, either as your full-time job or a weekend enterprise, also is part of the equation. The trigger for filing in this case is $400. If you are married and live in a community property state, half of any income your state law deems community earnings may be considered yours. This amount affects your federal filing requirement, even if you and your spouse do not file a joint return.

Filing status—In addition to inflation, the income amounts that determine whether you must file also vary depending upon your filing status. You can choose from single, married filing jointly, married filing separately, head of household, and widow or widower with a qualifying child.

In most instances, the required income amount for a single taxpayer is half that of a couple who sends in a joint return.

However, if a husband and wife decide to file separate returns, the income threshold for each is substantially lower. Why isn't it the same as single filers? In part, the tax laws want to reward joint filings because it makes the processing easier. Some tax benefits are not available to "married but separate filers," which makes things more complicated for taxpayers and IRS examiners alike.

A head of household taxpayer is one who is supporting others. Because of that, the income trigger amount for this status is a bit more than for single taxpayers. Similarly, a widow or widow raising at least one dependent child is allowed to earn even a bit more before he or she must submit a return.

Age—Finally, your age can affect whether you must file a return.

Youngsters are not automatically off the tax hook. When a child earns money, he or she must face the same tax consequences as other taxpayers. However, when a child is also the dependent of another taxpayer—that is, he or she can be claimed on another person's tax return for that person to obtain some additional tax benefits—different filing requirements apply.

A dependent filer must take into account both money earned from a job, as well as income from investments. How much income from each of those two sources determines whether the dependent must file his or her own tax return.

While dependents typically are children, a dependent could be an adult relative. And that dependent, regardless of age, much use the formula for determining whether he or she must file.

Older taxpayers, however, do receive some other special consideration when it comes to determining whether they must file.

If you are 65 or older, you are able to collect more gross income than other taxpayers before you must file.

Vision issues also can bump up the amount of money necessary to require filing. This extra income amount is calculated separately and could make a difference as to whether you must file, regardless of your age.

Other considerations—The general tax-filing requirements apply not only to U.S. citizens, whether living in America or abroad, but also to residents of Puerto Rico and resident aliens—that is, persons whose permanent residence is in the United States but who are not citizens.

Even if you don't have to file, sometimes it literally pays to do so. If you're due any refund amount or you're eligible for certain tax credits, submitting the proper paperwork to the IRS is the only way to get that money.

TRUTH

2

Figuring out your filing status

Every taxpayer's situation is unique. But the Internal Revenue Service gives us just five categories, or filing statuses, to choose from when we prepare our returns. They are single, married filling jointly, married filing separately, head of household, or qualifying widow or widower with a dependent child.

Given such limited choices, you would think picking the appropriate one would be a snap. It can be. But some of us need to take a little more time to ensure that we select the appropriate, and most tax-advantageous, status.

Your filing status is based on your marital status on the last day of the tax year. But, as is often the case when it comes to taxes, it's not that cut and dried. Some folks are able to file a couple of ways. Married couples can send in one 1040 or two. And the wrong choice could be quite costly.

Filing status, along with your income and age, helps determine whether you need to file a return at all. It's also a factor in your ability to claim certain tax breaks and determines just how much of a standard deduction you can claim.

Single—Single filing status is available to unmarried individuals. This is taxpayers who have never been married, are divorced, or are legally separated under a divorce or separate maintenance decree.

Remember, the last day of the tax year is the determinant. If you were married from Jan. 1 through Dec. 30, but your divorce is final on Dec. 31, you are considered unmarried for the full year.

Married filing jointly—Similarly, if your wedding was Dec. 31, you are considered married for that

> Filing status, along with your income and age, helps determine whether you need to file a return at all.

tax year and are able to file jointly. But you don't necessarily need a marriage certificate to qualify for this status. In addition to having a formal marriage certificate, the IRS also considers you married for tax purposes if, on the last day of the tax year, you are

- Living together in a common law marriage recognized by the state in which you live or by the state where the common law marriage began

- Married and living apart, but are not legally separated under your state's law

- Separated under an interlocutory—that is, not final—decree of divorce

In some cases, a marriage certificate is no good when it comes to filing jointly. Although same-sex marriages and civil unions are recognized by some states, federal law explicitly states that for IRS purposes, a marriage means only a legal union between a man and a woman as husband and wife.

If your spouse died before the end of the tax year and you did not remarry, you can still file a joint return for that year. Don't be confused by the qualifying widow/widower status; you'll find more on it in a few paragraphs.

Joint filing is the choice of most couples. Not only is it convenient for both you and your spouse, as well as the IRS, which then has to examine only one return for two people, you could lose some tax breaks if you file a separate return.

A joint return, however, does have some potential drawbacks.

When you and your spouse combine all your personal financial information on one form, you each are responsible for any tax that results, as well as for any possible tax penalty that might come from the combined filing. This shared tax liability applies even if only one spouse earned income.

Married filing separately—Because of potential tax troubles, some couples file separate returns. This is common when marriages are on the rocks or when one spouse suspects the other of using overly aggressive tax techniques.

But there are other, less sinister and potentially tax-cutting reasons to file two 1040s. For example, some tax breaks have limits that are easier for one, rather than two, taxpayers to meet.

Take medical deductions. To be claimed as an itemized deduction, medical expenditures must exceed 7.5 percent of a filer's adjusted gross income. If a couple makes a combined $100,000, this means they must have eligible health-related costs of more than $7,500 to get any tax break. But if the medical costs were primarily for the wife and her income alone was $40,000, her expenses over $3,000 would be deductible.

The goal is to use the filing status that produces the lowest combined tax.

Head of household—This filing status is a great benefit for single people with dependents.

When you provide more than half the cost of keeping up a home for yourself and a qualifying person who lived with you for more than six months, head of household status will get you a larger standard deduction. Your tax rate also will likely be lower than the rates for single or married filing separately taxpayers. In some cases, married persons living apart might qualify for this status.

Qualifying widow/widower—After you have lost a spouse and no longer are able to file a joint return as discussed earlier, if you still have children at home, look into this filing status. It essentially gives you the basic filing advantages (for example, larger standard deduction) of married joint filers.

The qualifying widow or widower status can be used for two years following the year a spouse passes away as long as the surviving spouse cares for a dependent child. The child must live in your home for the full tax year, and you must pay for more than half the cost of keeping up that home.

When a surviving spouse no longer qualifies for this status, he or she would file as a head of household if the kids are still living at home or, with no dependents to claim, as a single taxpayer.

TRUTH

3

Filling out the right form

1040. It's the most feared number in America, especially when April 15 is fast approaching.

Form 1040 is *the* tax document, the one millions of us complete to report our income and figure any associated federal taxes or refunds due.

There are, however, three 1040 versions. Picking the appropriate one could save you money.

Form 1040EZ—Because tax filing is a dreaded task, the allure of an official form labeled EZ is understandable. And for many people, this simplest of the three 1040 versions is the perfect filing answer.

But there are some restrictions. The main one is income, both the amount and type. You must make less than $100,000 to file the EZ. Even if you meet the income limit, if your earnings include interest of $1,500 or more, you cannot use the form. Neither is it available if you're living off of retirement account distributions.

Other 1040EZ prerequisites include the following:

- You be a single taxpayer or couple filing jointly.

- You have no dependents.

- You are younger than age 65. If you file a joint return, your spouse also must meet the age requirement. Be careful if you or your spouse were born on Jan. 1. In this case, for filing purposes the IRS considers you to have turned 65 the prior year, meaning you can't file the EZ form.

One thing that catches the eyes of many taxpayers is the 1040EZ's standard deduction amounts; they're larger than the amounts shown on the other two 1040s. Don't let that alone entice you to use the form; in reality, the standard deduction amounts are the same regardless of which 1040 version you use. The form simply combines the standard deduction and exemption amounts.

That's a nifty shortcut, but this form offers only one additional tax break, the earned income tax credit (EITC) that is designed for lower-income workers.

Form 1040A—Form 1040A is twice as long as 1040EZ, but it offers many more opportunities to save on taxes. It also can be used by taxpayers who file using any of the five filing statuses (single, married filing jointly, married filing separately, head of household, or qualifying widow/widower).

It does, however, have a few limitations. Your income must be less than $100,000. But you are

Form 1040A is twice as long as 1040EZ, but it offers many more opportunities to save on taxes.

allowed to report more interest and dividend income. When it comes to capital gains, though, only capital gains distributions, not profits or losses from the sale of assets, are allowed on this form.

Older taxpayers will find the 1040A more amenable. Pension and other retirement income can be reported on this form. Even better, the 1040A allows age 65 or older and visually impaired filers to claim a larger standard deduction. Elderly and disabled individuals also can claim a special credit on 1040A.

In addition, 1040A offers four income adjustments, also commonly called above-the-line deductions because they are found on page 1 of the form, just above where you enter your adjusted gross income, or AGI.

The 1040A above-the-line deductions that help reduce your taxable income are educator expenses, traditional IRA contributions, student loan interest, and higher education tuition and fees.

More tax-cutting options are available through seven credits found on Form 1040A. In addition to the EITC found on the EZ and the previously mentioned elderly or disabled credit, Form 1040A allows you to claim the child, additional child, education, dependent care, excess Social Security withholdings, and retirement savings credits.

Form 1040—If you want the most tax-saving chances, use the long Form 1040, the granddaddy of tax forms. It first appeared in 1913 just after ratification of the 16th Amendment, which gave Congress the authority to enact an income tax. Today's Form 1040 is packed with ways to report, and reduce, more types of income.

Form 1040 can be filed by a taxpayer using any filing status. It's required if your earnings are larger, you itemize deductions, or you have a variety of investment and other income, such as self-employment earnings, to report.

Form 1040 also is closely associated with another well-known piece of filing paperwork, Schedule A. This is the document used to itemize tax-deductible expenses, such as medical costs; home-related expenses (mortgage interest and property taxes); other taxes (state income or sales taxes); and charitable donations.

Some of these deductions are limited to certain percentages of your adjusted gross income. Your overall itemized deductions also might be reduced if you earn over a certain amount. But if you have enough allowable expenses to exceed the standard deduction amount available for your filing status, you should itemize. And that requires you to file the long Form 1040.

This longest form also offers more than a dozen above-the-line deductions. As with the 1040A, these tax breaks, officially called "adjustments to income," allow you to subtract certain amounts from your gross income. And although most people file Form 1040 because they itemize, you can claim above-the-line deductions regardless of whether you also file Schedule A.

In addition to the educator expenses, IRA contributions, student loan interest, and tuition and fees deductions found on the 1040A, the bottom of Form 1040's first page offers deductions for alimony payments, moving expenses, a portion of self-employment taxes, and contributions to certain self-employment retirement and various health savings accounts. Several specialized deductions also are found only on Form 1040. Details on each of the above-the-line deductions are found in the form's instruction book.

When you flip over the Form 1040, you'll find the tax-saving opportunities afforded by various credits. In addition to those found on the other two returns, Form 1040 offers the foreign tax credit and half a dozen specialty credits, such as breaks for electric and other alternative-fuel vehicles, prior-year minimum tax paid, and several business credits.

Of course, the additional tax-saving possibilities of the longer Form 1040A and Form 1040 require more time and extra schedules. But that price usually is more than offset by a reduction in your tax bill.

TRUTH

4

Meeting filing deadlines

The Internal Revenue Service is all about numbers, and that includes dates on calendars. If you don't file your return on time and if you owe tax, you'll face penalties and interest.

Everyone knows about April 15, the day tax returns are due. But as countless procrastinators can attest, it's when your return must be en route to the IRS, not when the agency actually has to have your 1040 in hand.

The IRS considers a paper return filed on time if it is mailed in a properly addressed envelope, has enough postage, and is postmarked by the due date. The official term, per Section 7502 of the Internal Revenue Code, is "timely filed." The tax code also notes that the date on a U.S. Postal Service receipt for certified or registered mail also qualifies.

As long as the tax mailing has the appropriate USPS cancellations showing it was mailed on or before the due date, the return is considered on time no matter when the IRS actually receives it.

Private delivery accepted—What if you're more comfortable using a private delivery service? That's okay with the IRS and has been since 1997.

In these cases, the IRS considers a timely-filed postmark to be the date a private delivery service records in its database that it accepted the tax document or marks that date on the mailing label.

The IRS has designated three companies as authorized private delivery services: DHL Express, Federal Express, and United Parcel Service. If you choose to use one of them, check with its local office as to the company's requirements and pick-up deadlines, as well as the specific private delivery services the IRS accepts.

Filing on time electronically—Electronic filing is popular in part because it enables you to send your 1040 from a personal computer with a simple push of the Enter button.

E-filing also provides an almost immediate acknowledgment that the return is on its way to Uncle Sam. This notification from tax software companies and other electronic return originators is your official electronic postmark.

Technically, an e-filed return is not considered filed until the IRS acknowledges that it has been received and accepted for processing.

However, if the electronic transmission is successful and completed on or shortly before the due date, the IRS considers it as timely filed.

But don't wait until 11:59 p.m. on April 15 to e-file. Although such a last-minute electronic timestamp is acceptable to the IRS, you run the risk that your online connection might be bogged down by other late e-filers. Worse, your PC could crash, not only causing you to miss the filing deadline, but also destroying your entire return.

> Technically, an e-filed return is not considered filed until the IRS acknowledges that it has been received and accepted for processing.

Pushing the deadline—Sometimes April 15 comes and goes without any tax consequence. That's the case when it falls on a weekend or federal holiday. In these instances, the next business day becomes the official tax-filing deadline.

The IRS also allows you, if you file the proper paperwork, six more months to complete your Form 1040. Submit Form 4868 by the regular April due date, and your filing deadline becomes October 15, or if that date falls on a weekend or federal holiday, the next business day.

Although an extension can be a welcome tax respite, keep in mind that it only gives you more time to file your return. It is not an extension of time to pay any tax you owe. Failure to pay will cause penalty and interest assessments to start accumulating.

There are three ways to file Form 4868:

1. Mail in the paper form, which can be downloaded from www.IRS.gov.

2. File it electronically. The form is included in most tax software packages, or eligible taxpayers can find it at the IRS's Free File site. Go to www.IRS.gov and type "Free File" in the search box at the top of the page.

3. Pay part or all of your tax bill by credit card via an authorized, private-sector service provider.

The IRS has authorized two companies to process credit cards payments:

- Link2Gov Corporation
  www.PAY1040.com
  1-888-729-1040

- Official Payments Corporation
  www.officialpayments.com
  1-800-272-9829

Both companies charge a convenience fee of 2.5 percent of the payment amount. And if you do not pay your full tax due, penalties and interest will accrue on the unpaid balance.

More filing deadlines for some—April 15, or the following business day if the 15th falls on a weekend or federal holiday, is a double deadline for some taxpayers. The mid-April date also is the due date for the year's first estimated tax payment.

U.S. taxes are collected on a pay-as-you-earn system, with the bulk of them paid by payroll withholding from employee wages. But when you are self-employed or have income, such as investment earnings, from which no taxes are withheld, you must make the payments yourself as estimated payments. If you do not pay enough throughout the year, either via withholding, estimated payments, or a combination of both, you could face an underpayment penalty.

To avoid this, Form 1040-ES, which includes instructions and payment vouchers, helps you calculate your untaxed income and figure your bill. The IRS prefers you take that total estimated amount, divide it by four, and send in equal payments on April 15, June 15, September 15 and January 15 of the following year. Again, holidays or weekends will push these deadlines to the next business day.

You can make each payment by sending the appropriate paper 1040-ES voucher, downloadable from www.IRS.gov; paying by credit card; having the funds electronically withdrawn from your bank account; or paying via the IRS's Electronic Federal Payment System, or EFTPS, at www.EFTPS.gov.

Figure your estimated payments carefully, since underpayment penalties also are assessed on each payment period if too little is remitted. If your income that is not subject to withholding is unequal throughout the year, you can avoid such penalties by using the annualized method. Using Form 2210, figure each 1040-ES payment period separately and pay the appropriate tax for each. This is particularly useful if your job is one where you earn most of your income in one period, such as a lawn service with key earnings during the summer, because you then will have the cash to pay the taxes.

TRUTH

5

Determining what's taxable

"If you make any money, the government shoves you in the creek once a year with it in your pockets, and all that don't get wet you can keep."
—*Will Rogers, humorist*

Sometimes it feels like the Internal Revenue Service taxes every single cent you make. The truth, however, is that our tax system is designed to provide you with ways to reduce the amount of money that Uncle Sam can touch.

Yes, the IRS does tax our income. But it also categorizes income in ways that allow us to lower our eventual tax bills. For tax purposes, your income is not just one amount. During the filing process, it is considered as three distinct types:

1. Total, or gross, income
2. Adjusted gross income, usually referred to as AGI
3. Taxable income

When you file, each income category is considered sequentially, and portions of your earnings are filtered out along the way. By the time you reach the end of your 1040, your taxable amount is less, and sometimes dramatically so, than the total income figure with which you began.

Total, or gross, income—The starting point for your eventual tax calculation is your total, or gross, income. And when the IRS says "total," that's what it means. It's essentially all the money from myriad sources that you receive during the tax year.

The most obvious is your wages or salary. Other compensation, such as commissions, fees, and tips also count. These amounts usually are reported to you, and the IRS, on your annual Form W-2, Wage and Tax Statement.

Some fringe benefits also might be included in your gross income, as are stock options and royalty payments from copyrights, patents, and oil, gas, and mineral properties.

Self-employment income, regardless of whether you operate your business as a sole proprietor, partnership, or corporation, is included in your gross income. Some self-employment income is reported, again to both you and the IRS, on a Form 1099-MISC. Even if you don't get a 1099, by law you must report all these earnings.

No job? No problem for the IRS. Unemployment benefits are considered income and you should get a 1099-G form detailing this reportable income.

If you're supplementing your wages with investment income, that will cost you, too. These earnings, be they from interest, dividends, or capital gains, are part of your total income. So are some retirement account payments, as is alimony you receive.

Don't try to circumvent the income definition by bartering.

Don't try to circumvent the income definition by bartering. You must include in your income the fair market value of property or services you receive for services you provide.

Some income that is credited or paid to you, but which you do not actually take possession of, also is part of your total income. This is known as constructively received income. One example of this is a check you get before the end of the tax year. Even if you don't cash it or deposit it until the next year, it is considered income in the year you got the check. Similarly, reinvested dividends or interest on your aforementioned investments also are counted as income in the year they are booked to your account, even though you do not actually touch the money that tax year.

Even money you don't get in some cases counts as income. Take the case of canceled debts. If a creditor agrees to write off part of what you owe, that amount of forgiven debt is usually considered income.

And if you're making money illegally, you need to start looking over your shoulder for IRS agents as well as local law enforcement. The feds don't care about your nefarious method, but they do want their share of your take. In fact, the IRS specifically states in Publication 525, "Illegal income, such as money from dealing illegal drugs, must be included in your income on Form 1040, line 21, or on Schedule C or Schedule C-EZ (Form 1040) if from your self-employment activity." Go ahead and laugh, but also remember that it was the failure to report ill-gotten gains that tripped up Al Capone.

Finally, there's that wonderful catch-all word "other." It appears on line 21 of Form 1040 telling you to report "other income." Common types of other income include certain distributions from educational or medical savings accounts, jury pay, and gambling winnings. And as Richard Hatch, the first winner of the Survivor television show discovered, you're also responsible for reporting any prizes you win.

After you add up all your total income, it's time to move on to your adjusted gross income.

Adjusted gross income, or AGI—You arrive at your AGI by subtracting certain amounts, technically known as adjustments but popularly referred to as above-the-line deductions, from your total income. You're able to use these deductions only by filing Form 1040A or 1040.

Above-the-line deductions get their name from their location on these tax returns. They are listed just above the final line on page one of both forms. Four of them—educator expenses, IRA contributions, student loan interest, and tuition and fees—are found on both the 1040A and 1040. The longer Form 1040 also enables you to subtract several other expenses, such as alimony payments to an ex-spouse, moving expenses, a portion of self-employment taxes, contributions to some retirement accounts, certain health-care related costs, as well as several specialized deductions.

After you subtract all applicable items, you have your AGI, which does several things.

It serves as an eligibility determinant for many tax breaks. If it's more than a certain amount, you'll lose the ability to claim some deductions or credits. And for tax calculation purposes, AGI also is the next step in figuring your taxable income amount.

Taxable income—As its name indicates, *taxable income* is the actual figure upon which your tax liability is based. The lower your taxable income, the lower your tax bill.

You whittle your AGI to the lowest possible taxable income level by subtracting personal exemptions, standard or itemized deduction amounts, and various credits.

Just how low you can get your taxable income depends on which tax breaks you're eligible to claim and, to a degree, which tax form you file. Ideally, by the time you complete whichever return you choose, you'll find that the amount of total income with which you began has morphed into a substantially lower taxable income amount.

TRUTH

6

Earned versus
unearned income

You work hard for your money, so it makes perfect sense that the tax code describes your pay as earned income.

But the IRS also taxes other money you make in ways not associated with your labor. This is known as *unearned income*.

The differentiation is important. The type of income could determine the tax rate you pay, whether you can claim certain tax breaks or, in some cases, whether you must file a return at all.

As the name indicates, earned income is any compensation in return for your labor. This includes wages, salaries, and self-employment earnings. Tips, bonuses, commissions, and some fringe benefits fall into this category. It doesn't matter whether the earnings are from a full-time or part-time job.

Unearned income, on the other hand, is any money you receive from sources other than your work. This includes such things as support and alimony payments; income from rental property; certain royalties; annuity, pension, or retirement benefits; disability, including workmen's compensation; unemployment insurance benefits; prizes and awards; death benefits; and certain trust distributions.

Unearned income tax rate benefits—Most taxpayers, however, encounter unearned income in connection with their investments. The interest from bonds, savings accounts, and other financial products, such as dividends from stocks and the capital gains you realize when you sell an asset, are considered unearned income.

Although some unearned income is taxed at regular income tax rates (this is the case with distributions from traditional IRAs and other tax-deferred retirement accounts), some of the unearned income from investments receives preferential tax treatment. Essentially, in these cases, lawmakers created a tax carrot to reward and encourage longer-term investments.

> Unearned income is any money you receive from sources other than your work.

Earned income is subject to the ordinary tax brackets, which range from 10 percent to 35 percent. But the unearned income produced by investments held for more than a year are taxed at substantially lower rates, 15 percent for most taxpayers. Some taxpayers could even avoid any taxes on these long-term holdings if they are in the lower tax brackets.

You must have earned income to open and contribute to either type of IRA.

Unearned income and tax breaks—Some tax breaks also depend on the type of income earned.

Tax advantages are afforded to both traditional and Roth individual retirement accounts. A traditional account allows some individuals an immediate tax deduction. This retirement account also enables contributions to grow tax-deferred. Roth IRAs have no immediate tax savings, but you can eventually take out the money without owing any tax on the earnings.

Although eligibility requirements vary slightly for traditional and Roth IRAs, they share one commonality. You must have earned income to open and contribute to either type of IRA.

Another popular tax break is the earned income tax credit (EITC). This is a federal tax program that reduces the amount of income tax owed by low- and moderate-income workers. Even people who don't make enough to owe income tax might be able to get a refund by claiming the EITC. In addition to the income threshold, as its name indicates, the EITC also requires that you have earned income to claim this credit. Because of this requirement, tax laws have been changed in some cases to allow individuals to count other income sources, such as military combat pay, as earned income so more filers can claim this credit.

And if you can be claimed as a dependent on another person's tax return, the amount of your earned income is a factor in determining just how much of a standard deduction you can claim on your own Form 1040.

Unearned income filing effects—The type of income you receive also could determine whether you must file a return at all.

Young investors, for example, do not have to file a tax return if their unearned income is the sole source of the money they receive and it is less than a certain threshold amount.

The amounts of earned and unearned income a person who is another's dependent also factor into whether that dependent has to file a return.

One other important distinction between earned and unearned income is how each is affected by the Federal Insurance Contributions Act, or FICA, which is the notation you see on your pay stub indicating withholding amounts that go to the Social Security and Medicare programs. In most cases, these withholding payments are collected only on earned income. Unearned income is not subject to FICA.

TRUTH
7

The alternative minimum tax

It's bad enough when you have to file and pay one tax bill. But each tax season, millions of taxpayers discover they are liable for a second, more costly levy: the alternative minimum tax.

This parallel tax system, commonly called the AMT, was created in 1969 to ensure that the well-to-do paid at least some tax. Back then, that meant a handful of taxpayers who earned $200,000 or more weren't allowed to claim some tax breaks.

Today, the AMT's reach goes beyond the wealthy. More middle-class taxpayers are finding they are the tax's prime target. The reason? Inflation. Over the last 40 years, wages have increased, but when lawmakers designed the AMT, they didn't build in the annual cost of living increasing price hikes.

The good AMT news is that for the last several years, federal lawmakers have recognized this flaw and passed legislation to reduce the tax's effect.

The bad AMT news is that the legislation is temporary. Each year, it must be renewed with new inflation-adjusted amounts. Without the annual fix, a projected 52 million taxpayers would face the AMT by 2015.

The worst AMT news is that piecemeal patches will likely continue. Congress routinely talks about repealing the AMT, but even with its effect reduced by the annual tweaks, the system still brings in millions of dollars that Washington, DC, is loathe to forfeit. When taxpayers do have to pay the AMT, federal data shows that on average they pay around $2,000 more than they would have under the regular tax system.

Two sets of rules, calculations—The AMT is a second taxing system with its own set of rates, 26 percent and 28 percent. Affected taxpayers must calculate both their regular tax and what they owe under the alternative system and then pay the higher of the two figures.

The great irony of the AMT is that it doesn't usually affect higher-income filers, the group for whom it was created. Those taxpayers escape the AMT because they tend to pay more under the regular tax system thanks to its two top tax brackets of 33 percent and 35 percent.

Adding insult to potential tax bill injury, taxpayers must complete additional paperwork in connection with the AMT. Even if you ultimately escape the added tax, you're out the time it took to figure your possible AMT bill.

The IRS has an interactive program at www.IRS.gov to help in this regard. Using information from your Form 1040, you answer some questions, and the online calculator will tell you whether you're off the AMT hook or need to file Form 6251 to figure your AMT. The IRS program is especially useful if you still use paper forms and rely on the agency's worksheet. If you use tax preparation software, it should run the numbers for you.

Will it affect you?—Upon learning about the alternative minimum tax, the first question usually is how do you know if it applies to you? There's not an easy answer. Several factors can trigger the AMT, and because each taxpayer's situation is unique, there's no one AMT template. There are, however, some general guidelines.

The first indicator that AMT might apply is your taxable income. Lawmakers set a threshold amount for each filing status with regard to the AMT. If your taxable income for regular tax purposes, plus any adjustments and preference items that you have to add back, are more than your AMT exemption amount, you might have to pay the extra tax.

Next, look at the various tax breaks you claim. The AMT eliminates or reduces many of these, thereby increasing your tax liability. Some common tax breaks on your regular return that could cause you to owe AMT include the following:

> Several factors can trigger the AMT, and because each taxpayer's situation is unique, there's no one AMT template.

- **A large number of exemptions**—The exemptions you claim for yourself, your spouse, and your dependents are not allowed under AMT, meaning that large families are particularly vulnerable.

- **The standard deduction**—Most filers use this deduction rather than itemize, but it's not allowed under the AMT. When that write-off is removed, it could push you into AMT territory.

- **State and local taxes**—If your state's taxes are high, they could pose AMT problems because you're not allowed to deduct them under that system. This includes both state and local income taxes, as well as your home's property taxes.

- **Medical expenses**—To be claimed under AMT, these costs must meet a higher threshold, 10 percent of your adjusted gross income versus 7.5 percent under regular tax.

- **Second mortgage interest**—Your main home loan interest is okay, but if you took out another loan using your home as collateral, that loan's interest cannot be deducted under the AMT.

- **Incentive stock options**—Exercising these options usually doesn't pose a regular tax problem, but under the AMT it will cost you, since the spread between the purchase and grant price is subject to the parallel tax.

- **Various credits**—Some regular tax credits aren't allowed, so the more you claim, the greater your chance of owing AMT.

Avoiding the AMT—Unfortunately, because you typically don't know you owe it until you file your 1040, it's just as difficult to map out an AMT avoidance strategy. You can, however, take some general preventative measures.

If you suspect you might owe AMT, consider accelerating ordinary income into this year and deferring tax breaks, such as state and local income and real estate taxes, into the next year. This is contrary to the usual tax advice, but it could prevent you from paying AMT and ultimately save you some tax dollars.

Finally, keep in mind that if you're subject to the AMT, you also could face penalties and interest because you didn't factor in the added tax when you figured your withholding exemptions or estimated tax payments. So, if it looks like you might owe the parallel tax, adjust your regular tax payroll withholding as soon as possible to cover any shortfall. The IRS has created an online tool to help you determine whether you might face the AMT; just type "AMT assistant" into the search box at IRS.gov.

8

Our progressive tax system

progressive tax structure really means to their tax bill. And most don't realize that they are paying less in taxes than they think.

Progressivity simply means the more you earn, the more taxes you pay. Our tax system currently has six income tax brackets, and as the money you receive "progresses" through them, your tax rate increases.

But that also has some advantages.

The brackets are allocated by filing status, and each year the income ranges to which each tax rate applies are adjusted for inflation. For illustration purposes, let's look at the 2008 numbers.

	Filing Statuses			
Tax Rates	**Single**	**Head of Household**	**Married Filing Jointly or Qualifying Widow/ Widower**	**Married Filing Separately**

The portion of your earnings that are in the 10 percent bracket are taxed at that lowest rate. As your income progresses through the brackets, the amounts that fall into those other brackets are taxed at those applicable rates.

Ultimately, the last few dollars of your income is taxed at 28 percent. But thanks to the fact that your tax bill is computed over four progressive tax brackets, the highest rate into which your income fell, 28 percent, actually applied to the least amount of your earnings.

Using your tax bracket to plan tax savings—Knowing your marginal tax rate can help you develop strategies to help reduce your eventual tax bill.

For example, you can determine what a raise costs you in taxes. For example, a salary bump increases your total income to $90,000. You're still well within the 28 percent bracket, but that extra income will add to the amount of money taxed at your highest, marginal rate and push up your tax bill somewhat.

You're not likely to turn down your raise because you'll owe a bit more in taxes, but by figuring the tax bite, you can take steps to make it less painful. You can increase your contributions to your company 401(k) plan. Because this retirement plan money is put into your account before taxes are figured, you'll be able to keep your raise but move it to a tax-deferred position where it won't cost you so much during the current tax year.

If your wage hike is in the form of a bonus, talk with your employer about pushing back receipt of that money until the next year if that will help soften the tax blow.

You also can consider increasing your deductions. As a 28-percent tax bracket taxpayer, every dollar you deduct will save you 28 cents. Perhaps your raise means you know you can afford to buy a home and take advantage of the mortgage interest deduction to help lower your tax bill.

> You're not likely to turn down your raise because you'll owe a bit more in taxes, but by figuring the tax bite, you can take steps to make it less painful.

Investments also are affected by your marginal tax rate.

Investments also are affected by your marginal tax rate. Stocks that you've held for a year or less, for example, are taxed at your ordinary tax rate. So, any profit you make on the sale of a short-term asset will be taxed at your marginal rate. Also be aware of the possibility that the transaction could even push you into the next tax bracket.

By knowing your marginal tax rate and how it affects your earnings, you can keep an eye on your money, its tax implications, and how you can manage them.

TRUTH

Why credits are better

Taxpayers have gotten a lot smarter over the years. Once, the filing-day tax cry was "Deduct!"

Now folks know they usually can save more tax dollars by claiming tax credits.

There are several reasons why credits tend to come out on top when you're looking for tax savings.

The main reason is that in tax parlance, "credit" means the same thing as it does when you see that line item on your charge account statement. A tax credit is a dollar-for-dollar benefit. The credit is applied to your final IRS bill, meaning you get money back or don't have to pay Uncle Sam as much.

A tax deduction, however, reduces the taxable income upon which your final tax bill is figured. Less income usually means a smaller tax bill but generally not as much as does a credit.

You can get an idea of the value of credits by comparing the tax savings of an ostensibly larger deduction to that of a credit.

The tuition and fees deduction offers eligible taxpayers a $4,000 deduction. Another tax break for educational expenses, the Lifetime Learning credit, is only half that. But don't be so fast to opt for the deduction.

With the $4,000 deduction, you subtract that amount from your earnings to reach a smaller taxable income amount; $50,000 then becomes $46,000. But that $46,000 still leaves you in the 25 percent tax bracket, meaning that your $4,000 deduction is worth, when you finally compute your tax bill, only a fourth of its dollar value: $4,000 × 25 percent, or $1,000.

The $2,000 Lifetime Learning credit, however, is subtracted from your final tax bill. So if you owed $2,200 on your $50,000 income, the credit will knock that down to only $200.

Credit ebb and flow—In recent years, as lawmakers have looked to provide more breaks for constituent taxpayers, a number of credits have been added to the tax code. Congress sometimes adds them temporarily; other times, it makes the breaks permanent.

But in each case, the guiding principal is the same. While deductions, whether itemized or the standard amount, help you whittle down the amount of income upon which your tax bill is figured, credits will cut your final IRS tab dollar-for-dollar, and in some cases even provide you a refund after you've zeroed out your bill.

And some popular core credits have stood the test of time and taxpayers. These include credits to give you a break for caring for, or simply having, children, saving for retirement, furthering your or a family member's education, and even recouping Social Security overpayments.

Refundable versus nonrefundable—Although credits generally are preferable to deductions, some credits have greater tax appeal than others.

There are two types of tax credits: refundable and nonrefundable. Again, this is a case where the IRS actually means what it says.

A *refundable credit* means that the tax break will get you money back from the IRS even if your tax bill is zero. For example, you owe $500 and can claim a $1,000 tax credit. If that credit is refundable, you'll get $500 back as a refund.

However, if the credit is nonrefundable, you'll only be able to use the credit to zero out your tax bill, but no more than that. The excess $500 from the credit is lost.

As you have likely surmised, most tax credits are nonrefundable. The major, and most popular, credits in this category are the following:

- Child Tax credit, which can be claimed by parents of young children.

- Child and Dependent Care credit, available to working parents.

- Credit for the Elderly or Disabled, which provides tax savings to folks age 65 or older or to disabled taxpayers of any age.

- Retirement Savings Contributions credit, which encourages individuals to build their nest eggs.

- Adoption credit, offering additional tax help when you add to your family.

- Hope and Lifetime Learning credits, to help taxpayers and their families further their educations.

Only three permanent credits offer you the chance at a refund, as follows:

- Earned Income Tax credit, created for lower-income workers.

- Additional Child Tax credit, which some taxpayers can file for after claiming the basic Child Tax credit.

- Credit for taxes withheld on wages and other amounts, which helps employees recover Social Security withholding amounts that exceeded the statutory limit.

These are just a few of the more popular tax credits. Every year, federal lawmakers find room in the tax code for a few more credits. These usually are limited to very specific situations, such as the purchase of an alternative-fuel vehicle, and tend to be temporary.

But it's worth the time and effort to take a look at your tax form—the long Form 1040 gives you the most complete picture of available tax breaks—to see if a credit might help reduce your tax bill.

Tax credit limits—While claiming credits generally is the wiser tax move, even they have their limits.

Many credits are reduced or even unavailable for taxpayers who earn over certain income thresholds. Some of these limits are set by statute; others are adjusted periodically for inflation.

In many cases, age and filing status also are a factor in a taxpayer's ability to claim a credit.

Because the IRS frowns on double-dipping, you must be careful to coordinate your tax credit claims with other possible tax benefits.

Many credits are reduced or even unavailable for taxpayers who earn over certain income thresholds.

If you believe a tax credit could be useful, be sure to double-check its eligibility parameters. In some cases, such as with the Earned Income Tax Credit, the IRS web site (www.IRS.gov) offers interactive programs to help you determine your tax-break eligibility.

One final note about credits. Although you tend to see them paired off against deductions when the value of each is discussed, the use of these tax breaks is not an either/or situation.

You can claim every available tax deduction for which you qualify and also utilize as many tax credits for which you're eligible. The combination of the two is a great way to get your tax bill to its lowest possible level.

You can claim every available tax deduction for which you qualify and also utilize as many tax credits for which you're eligible.

TRUTH

10

Standard versus itemized deductions

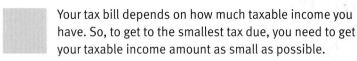Your tax bill depends on how much taxable income you have. So, to get to the smallest tax due, you need to get your taxable income amount as small as possible.

One way to accomplish this is by claiming deductions. Most of us have a choice of taking either the standard deduction amount or itemizing allowable expenses. And most of us use the standard deduction.

Internal Revenue Service annual filing statistics for the last few years have shown that around two-thirds of filers claim the standard amount. One of the main reasons for the choice is that it's easy. There's no need to keep track of, or justify if the IRS has questions, your actual deductions, such as medical expenses, charitable contributions, and state and local income, property, or sales taxes.

The standard deduction also is appealing because the amount you can claim is listed directly on each of the three tax forms: the 1040, 1040A, and 1040EZ. But look carefully at the amounts on the forms. Just how much of a standard deduction you can claim depends on your filing status.

Different amounts for different taxpayers—Although it's called the standard deduction, there are several possible deduction amounts. The one that you can claim depends on several factors.

The largest standard deduction goes to married couples who file a joint return. Thanks to tax-law changes in 2003, this standard deduction amount now is twice that of single filers. The standard deduction for husbands and wives who file separate returns is the same as that for single taxpayers. Although head-of-household taxpayers are single individuals, these folks get a slightly larger standard deduction because they are taking care of dependents.

The deduction amounts for each filing status are increased each year to account for inflation.

Taxpayers who are age 65 or older or who are legally blind get a slightly larger standard deduction. In a few cases, however, your standard deduction might be lower than the usual amount. This could happen if another person, such as a parent, can claim an exemption for you on his or her tax return.

Also, keep in mind the phrase "most people have a choice" when it comes to claiming the standard deduction or itemizing. There are some situations when you must itemize, such as you are married, filing a separate return, and your spouse itemizes deductions or you are a nonresident or dual-status alien during the tax year.

The many itemized deductions—For the other 30 percent of taxpayers each year, the Schedule A is their best tax friend. On this form, you enter your eligible deductible expenses in seven categories:

■ Medical and dental expenses

■ Taxes you paid

■ Interest you paid

■ Gifts to charity

■ Casualty and theft losses

■ Job expenses and certain miscellaneous deductions

■ Other miscellaneous deductions

As the deduction categories indicate, you might benefit from itemizing your eligible expense if you had large expenses in any of these areas.

However, don't just assume that a large dollar amount for any allowable itemized deduction will automatically help cut your tax bill. Some of the deductions on that form are available only if you have enough to meet certain thresholds.

For example, your medical expenses must exceed 7.5 percent of your adjusted gross income. The costs you incur related to your job and other miscellaneous expenses, such as costs related to investment or tax preparation fees, must exceed 2 percent of your AGI.

If you do not meet these required amounts, your itemized deductions

> Don't just assume that a large dollar amount for any allowable itemized deduction will automatically help cut your tax bill.

in these categories are of no use. And that could mean that your total itemized deductions aren't enough to exceed the standard amount you can claim. So it's important to run the Schedule A numbers to make sure that filing this form is worth the extra trouble.

In fact, you should review your possible deductions periodically throughout the tax year. If you find that your itemized deduction total will likely come up just short of exceeding your standard amount, you will have time to make the moves, such as increasing your deductible charitable contributions or paying a state tax bill early, to push your itemized expenses over the standard top. If you wait until the very end of the tax year to compare your deduction options, it could be too late to make adjustments that could help your tax situation.

Making the right choice—If you have a choice, you should use the deduction method that gives you the lower tax. In most cases, that's the option that produces the larger deduction amount. But that's not always the case.

The conventional deduction wisdom could work against you—for example, if you find you will owe alternative minimum tax. Under the alternative minimum tax, usually referred to as the AMT, you have to add back your standard deduction amount when figuring the parallel tax amount due. But if you have some AMT allowable itemized deductions, such as mortgage interest or charitable contributions, even though they are smaller than your standard amount, you will at least be able to claim them against your AMT liability.

Also, remember that your deduction method choice is not permanent. You can change it every filing season to produce the best tax result for that tax year. In fact, some taxpayers find that itemizing one year, then claiming the standard deduction the next, is a good way to cut their tax bills. This is possible because they bunch their itemized expenses into one tax year to claim an amount larger than their standard deduction; then the following year, when they don't have those expenses to claim, they use the standard amount.

By understanding the advantages and limitations of each deduction method and paying a little bit of attention throughout the tax year, you'll be able to maximize your deductions and more effectively lower your tax liability.

TRUTH

11

Dealing with deduction limitations

Each year, around a third of taxpayers find that itemizing their deductions is the best way to reduce their tax bill. They hang onto receipts and carefully transfer amounts to Schedule A to come up with a figure that's more than the standard deduction amount.

But sometimes, the extra work doesn't pay off. Some itemized expenses are worthless because they don't meet specific threshold limits. And even the total itemized amount could be cut when a filer's income is too large.

Medical expenses—Many types of medical expenses are deductible on Schedule A. But to claim them, they must add up to more than 7.5 percent of your adjusted gross income (AGI).

For example, if your AGI is $100,000, your itemized medical deductions must exceed $7,500. The key word here is "exceed." If you rack up $7,499 in deductible medical costs, they are of no use on Schedule A. And if you have $8,000 in medical expenses to itemize, only $500, the amount that exceeds your 7.5 percent threshold, is deductible.

> Some itemized expenses are worthless because they don't meet specific threshold limits.

There are, however, many expenses you can claim, including those for your spouse if you file a joint return and any dependents, to ensure that you exceed your deductible threshold. The most common costs are co-payments for physician visits and prescriptions, but you also can include medical insurance premiums as long as you paid them with already taxed dollars, as well as some long-term care policy costs.

Other deductible medical treatments include those that are often not covered by insurance, such as eyeglasses, false teeth, and hearing aids. Medically prescribed weight loss treatments are allowed, as are stop-smoking programs. And certain home renovations also can be written off on Schedule A if they are required to treat or ease a medical condition.

Although the list of allowable medical deductions is wide ranging, the IRS frowns on some treatments. Purely cosmetic surgery is not deductible. Neither are health club dues or over-the-counter medications. A complete list of what can and cannot be written off is included in the IRS Publication 502.

Most filers are able to deduct all their gifts to IRS-authorized charities.

That document is worth perusing. It could help you plan, when practicable, medical treatments to take full advantage of their tax value. If you're close to reaching the 7.5 percent requirement, consider scheduling qualified medical treatments, such as a child's orthodontia or Lasik eye surgery, to help you qualify. On the other hand, if you find that you won't be anywhere near your threshold in a tax year, defer nonessential medical treatments into the next one when you might be able to deduct them.

Charitable gifts—Most filers are able to deduct all their gifts to IRS-authorized charities. However, if you're excessively generous, you could run into a donation limit. In most cases, cash gifts (which also includes donations by credit card checks) or the value of goods contributed to a charity are not deductible if the total comes to more than 50 percent of your AGI. The limit is lower, 30 percent, if you donate assets such as stocks, bonds, or other propriety on which you would have paid capital gains tax. And in some cases, the income limit is 20 percent, depending on the type of charitable organization. You can carry forward excess donations and claim them on future tax returns for up to five years.

Casualty and theft losses—The tax code offers some help if you suffer losses, but there are limits. First, you subtract any insurance payments you received or expect to get in connection with the loss of or damage to your home, household items, and vehicles. The remaining amount then must be more than $100. Finally, your loss must be more than 10 percent of your AGI.

Job expenses and certain miscellaneous expenses—In the job expenses Schedule A section, you can include unreimbursed job expenses that are necessary for you to do your job, such as uniform costs or professional membership dues. If you find you're paying too many of these types of costs and want to find another position in your career field, you can write off many of those job-hunting costs here, too. Even tax preparation costs, for computer software or accountant's fees, can be deducted in this section of Schedule A.

> There is no percentage limitation on gambling losses, but they are restricted to the amount that matches your winnings.

These miscellaneous amounts, however, must be more than 2 percent of your AGI. The Schedule A instructions and IRS Publication 529 list the miscellaneous deductions you can and cannot claim. A review of that inventory will help you determine whether you should renew some memberships or professional journal subscriptions this tax year or postpone them into another year when you'll have enough to exceed the 2 percent threshold.

Gambling losses—If you were lucky in Las Vegas, unfortunately, you can't leave the tax implications there. You must report your winnings as other income. However, you can reduce the tax bite of your good fortune by deducting gambling losses in the "Other Miscellaneous Deductions" section of Schedule A.

There is no percentage limitation on gambling losses, but they are restricted to the amount that matches your winnings. Essentially, you can zero out your winnings in a tax year, but you cannot create an income loss based on the bad hands you drew. The good news is that if you won $10,000 at a poker game, you don't have to use just poker losses to reduce those winnings. You can count blackjack, craps, and roulette table losses, as well as horse or dog racing bad bets and lottery tickets that didn't pay off.

Overall Schedule A limit—Finally, even if you meet all these limits, you still could lose some of your itemized deduction total if your AGI exceeds a certain limit. Check the last section of the form for the figure, which is adjusted annually for inflation. Then you'll have to complete a worksheet to determine exactly how much or an itemized deduction amount you can transfer to your Form 1040 and subtract to reach a lower taxable income level.

TRUTH

12

Maximizing charitable deductions

Giving to your favorite charity can pay off at tax time as long as you know and follow IRS rules.

The first requirement is that you itemize. If you claim the standard deduction, which most taxpayers do, your generosity will benefit your favorite charity, but it won't help reduce your tax liability.

Next, make sure you give to an IRS-qualified charity. A running list of authorized groups is contained in IRS Publication 78, with a searchable version on www.IRS.gov. You also can verify an organization's tax-exempt status by asking to see its IRS authorization letter, or by calling the IRS toll-free at 1-877-829-5500.

You also need to be aware of potential limitations. In most cases, as long as your total donations don't exceed half of your adjusted gross income, you're okay. If you plan to contribute unusually large amounts, check with your tax adviser and the charity about any possible tax implications.

Now to the actual giving.

Documentation rules—You can contribute cash or goods. In tax talk, "cash" includes not just currency, but also checks, electronic transfers, money orders, and charge payments.

The tax code now requires that all monetary donations be substantiated by a bank record or written receipt from the charity. A canceled check will serve as the requisite record, so will a credit card statement. Many charities already provide receipts for monetary gifts, regardless of the amount. If your favorite nonprofit doesn't automatically do so, ask for one when you donate. For donations of $250 or more, you must get an official receipt.

You don't have to send in the documentation with your return, but if the IRS asks and you can't produce acceptable verification, your gift could be disallowed.

If your contribution entitles you to merchandise (for example, the CDs and such that PBS stations offer during pledge periods) or admission to a special event (such as a charity

In tax talk, "cash" includes not just currency but also checks, electronic transfers, money orders, and charge payments.

ball), you can deduct only the amount that exceeds the fair market value of the benefit you receive.

Noncash contributions—Record-keeping requirements for noncash gifts depend on the value of the contributed goods. The major consideration here is donation of items valued at more than $5,000. For these higher-priced gifts, you generally must obtain a written appraisal of the property.

In addition to specific documentation rules, the IRS has certain deduction and filing requirements for donated goods.

You must fill out Section A of Form 8283 if your total deduction for all noncash contributions is more than $500. When your donated property amount exceeds $5,000, in addition to an appraisal, you also must complete Section B of Form 8283.

As for the property itself, tax law now requires that any donated household items be in good or better condition. If they're not, the IRS could disallow your contribution. The key here is to use the true fair market value of your gift. There are several software programs that can help you figure this out, as well as IRS Publication 561. Also check online auction sites for the going price for an item you plan to donate.

The condition-of-goods clause was added in 2006 to eliminate two problems:

1. Taxpayers using charitable groups as de facto garbage dumps.

2. The loss of government money because of overvalued donations.

The obvious question is how will the IRS know the condition of your donated goods? An auditor won't, but he or she will look closely at claims, and the law now gives examiners more leeway to ask questions if they see what they deem is an usually large charitable contribution amount on a Schedule A.

Vehicle donations—Tax revenue lost to overvalued donations also was why lawmakers toughened vehicle donation rules.

You no longer can automatically deduct the Blue Book value of your donated jalopy. Instead, you must take into account the value of your auto, as well as what the charity does with it. The organization has to let you know how the vehicle was or is used and, if it was sold, at what price.

Most vehicular donations are autos, but these contribution rules also apply to boats, airplanes, and other motorized vehicles. When you give a charitable group any of these machines, you'll need to file Form 1098-C with your tax return.

Often-overlooked gifts—There are several other tax-deductible ways to contribute.

You can write off the cost of gas and oil used in going to and from an organization at which you volunteer. If you prefer, rather than track actual costs, you can deduct 14 cents for each mile. You also can deduct travel expenses incurred while you were away from home performing services for a charitable group.

The cost of buying and cleaning uniforms used in volunteer work is deductible. So are some out-of-pocket expenses, such as stationery and stamps you purchased so that your favorite nonprofit could send out a mailing.

If you own appreciated stock that no longer fits your portfolio goals, consider giving it to a charity. Not only will you get to deduct the equity's value at the time it was donated, but also you will avoid capital gains on its appreciated value.

Contributions you can't deduct—You already know that donations must be made to IRS-qualified groups to be deductible. The IRS also has some specific instances when giving isn't deductible. You cannot write off contributions to individuals, such as a fund to help a family experiencing hardship. Neither can you deduct the value of your time spent volunteering or services you provided the group at no cost.

Timing is everything—Finally, remember that your donations are deductible in the tax year in which you make them.

For example, if you pledged $500 to a charity in September but paid only $200 by Dec. 31, your deduction for that tax year is $200. You can deduct credit card charges and payments by check in the year they are made or mailed, even if you do not pay your credit card bill or your check doesn't clear your bank account until the following year.

Donations of goods, however, must be in the charity's possession by the end of the tax year.

TRUTH

13

Deducting without itemizing

Most taxpayers claim the standard deduction. But every tax-filing season, these folks tend to get overlooked since the focus is on tax tips for those who itemize deductions.

Yes, there is a lot to be covered for Schedule A filers. But even taxpayers who take the standard deduction have a chance to lower their tax bills by claiming what are popularly known as above-the-line deductions.

These technically are adjustments to income. They're found in the section titled Adjusted Gross Income at the bottom of the first page of Form 1040. A few also show up in the same section on Form 1040A.

The above-the-line label comes because the total of these adjustments is tallied just before the last line of both forms.

Those lines on which the deductions are listed are pretty constant, although in some years the IRS is forced to make tweaks because Congress is slow in reauthorizing some of the deductions that periodically expire. Regardless of the exact location on the forms, each deduction offers you, if you're eligible, additional ways to shave some dollars off your total income. This, in turn, will give you a lower adjusted gross income amount and eventually less taxable income and a lower tax bill.

The above-the-line tax breaks include such things as education-related costs (for teachers as well as students), retirement and health plan contributions, and moving expenses. They are available to every eligible taxpayer, even those who itemize. But they are especially welcomed by filers who don't use Schedule A, since these above-the-line options represent a sort of side-door into the tax deduction room that, until now, you've been locked out of.

Here's a look at the above-the-line deductions that typically appear on Form 1040 and, to a lesser degree, on Form 1040A.

Educator expenses—This is where teachers and other employees of public and private schools, grades Kindergarten through 12, can write off up to $250 of personal money spent on classroom supplies. This deduction is one that is temporary, but which has the support not only of taxpayers but also lawmakers and is routinely renewed by Congress. It appears on both Form 1040 and Form 1040A.

Tuition and fees—With this tax break, you can subtract to $4,000 of qualified education costs from your total income. The educational expenses can be for you, your spouse, or a dependent. This above-the-line deduction also must be extended when it expires, but like the educator expenses tax break, it has widespread legislative support. It also can be claimed on the 1040A as well as the long 1040.

Student loan interest—If you are paying a college loan, you can deduct up to $2,500 in interest you paid on that debt. This deduction is on both Form 1040 and Form 1040A.

IRA deduction—Although the traditional IRA usually takes a back seat to the Roth account, some individuals still have these old-style retirement plans. If you're one of these account holders, you might be able to deduct contributions to your traditional IRA directly on your Form 1040 or Form 1040A.

Moving expenses—Under certain circumstances, many of your relocation costs can be deducted from your gross income directly on Form 1040.

Self-employment expenses—On Form 1040, you'll find several lines that will let you subtract some of the costs of doing business. You can deduct one-half of the self-employment tax that you pay. If you contribute to a qualified self-employment retirement plan, that amount is an allowed adjustment to your gross income, as are premiums you paid for your own health insurance policy.

Alimony—If you're paying support to an ex-spouse, you can write it off as an above-the-line deduction. Note that this is for spousal payments only; you cannot deduct child support.

Health savings accounts—These accounts, usually referred to as health savings accounts (HSAs), are medical coverage plans in which you establish an IRA-like account. Money you put in that account is deductible.

Penalty on early withdrawal of savings—If you had to cash in a CD

> On Form 1040, you'll find several lines that will let you subtract some of the costs of doing business.

and paid the price at your bank, you now can write off that fee as an above-the-line deduction.

Certain business expenses—This above-the-line write-off is designed to help very specific job categories—military reservists, performing artists, and fee-based government officials. If that's you, you can deduct eligible expenses. Other workers must still use Schedule A miscellaneous deductions (with its 2 percent threshold) to claim their work-related costs.

Domestic production activities—This is another business tax break, created to reward certain businesses that put the "made in the U.S.A." label on their products. It allows eligible taxpayers in the construction, farming, and some artistic fields to write off some of the costs of keeping their production efforts within U.S. borders.

Other deductions—Although it's not noted on the form itself, you can claim several other expenses on the Form 1040 line where you total your above-the-line deductions. Many are obscure and limited to very specific situations, but a review of the Form 1040 instructions lets you know that you might be able to deduct things such as jury pay (under certain circumstances), as well as contributions to some medical savings accounts.

It always pays
to check out the
form instructions,
because
sometimes
the available
above-the-line
deductions
change, or appear
elsewhere.

It always pays to check out the form instructions, because as noted earlier, sometimes the available above-the-line deductions change, or appear elsewhere, depending on Congressional actions. Also, some of these deductions have eligibility requirements, such as income limits or filing status conditions.

You also might have to complete added worksheets or other tax forms to claim some above-the-line deductions, but that extra time could be well worth it in tax savings.

TRUTH

14

Marriage and taxes

"Like mothers, taxes are often misunderstood, but seldom forgotten."

—Lord Bramwell,
Nineteenth-century English jurist

You've tied the knot, but when it comes to taxes, you definitely don't want to encounter any knotty problems.

Not to worry. True, there definitely are some specific tax considerations for married filers. And some taxpayers might find they are paying slightly bigger tax bills. But marriage also offers many tax advantages.

Filing status—Your wedding date is as important to the IRS as it is to you. For filing purposes, you are married for the full tax year as long as you exchange vows by December 31.

After you're married, you can send in your returns jointly or as married filing separately. Most couples prefer the joint option, but depending upon your particular financial and tax circumstances, separate filings could be warranted.

Joint filing typically is a good idea if you both work and one makes considerably more than the other. Combining incomes could bring the higher earnings into a lower tax bracket. Some tax credits are only available to a married couple when they file a joint return. And logistically, it's easier to deal with just one return.

Separate returns might be preferable if one spouse has large medical bills and can meet the deduction threshold by considering only his or her income. Other itemized deduction thresholds (miscellaneous deductions or casualty losses) also could be easier for just one partner to meet.

Keep in mind, though, that if one spouse itemizes on his or her separate return, the other spouse also must itemize. That could pose a costly problem for a spouse who has no or few itemized expenses and would be better off claiming the standard deduction.

Separate filing also is recommended when a spouse has concerns about tax claims the other wants to make. In most situations, when couples file jointly, each

> Separate returns might be preferable if one spouse has large medical bills and can meet the deduction threshold by considering only his or her income.

partner accepts equal responsibility for any tax due or penalties that might be assessed if problems arise with the return.

Some couples actually enjoy a marriage bonus.

Marriage penalty or bonus—One penalty of concern to couples has nothing to do with tax return mistakes. It's the marriage penalty, where some dual-income couples find that their combined tax bill is larger than it would have been if they were still filing singly.

However, tax law changes since 2001 (and in effect through 2010) have eased the possible penalty. The standard tax deduction for joint filers is now double that of a single taxpayer. More important, the maximum income in 10 percent and 15 percent tax brackets for joint filers is now double that of a single filer. That effectively means that couples in these brackets are taxed as if they were still single taxpayers.

Despite the changes, some couples still could face a bit of marriage penalty. This occurs when their combined earnings push them into the four higher brackets (25 percent, 28 percent, 33 percent, and 35 percent), where the income amounts are not strictly doubled.

And some couples actually enjoy a marriage bonus. This is often the case when there is a large difference between a husband's and wife's incomes.

Home sale tax advantage—A home is a major acquisition, regardless of marital status. But when a married couple sells their residence, they get a tax break that is twice as large as that available to single home sellers. By living in the property for at least two of the five years before selling, a couple can exclude from tax up to $500,000 in sale profits versus $250,000 for single sellers.

The larger home sale exclusion remains even after a spouse passes away. As long as the surviving spouse remains unmarried and sells the couple's home within two years of the day his or her spouse died, the widow or widower can claim the $500,000 joint gain exclusion.

Estate tax advantages—Estate taxes are a concern for all filers, but the good news is that the Internal Revenue Code exempts millions of dollars of assets from this tax. The better news for married couples is that they don't have to worry about limits. You can leave an estate worth any amount to your spouse and, thanks to what is known as the estate tax marital deduction, there are no federal estate taxes to pay.

Estate assets left to a spouse aren't tax-free. Rather, potential taxes are deferred. But the estate tax marital deduction gives the surviving spouse time to make other tax moves to ease taxes on the eventual distribution of the assets to heirs.

Surviving spouse filing status—After the loss of a spouse, you'll need to sort through filing status issues. If you remain unmarried in the year that your husband or wife died, you can file your tax return jointly, taking into account your deceased spouse's income. This allows you to take advantage of the larger standard deduction and potential credit claims. If you do remarry within that tax year, in addition to filing your joint (or married filing separately) return with your new spouse, be sure to file your deceased spouse's tax return.

If you have dependent children and remain unmarried, the next tax year you should file as a qualifying widow or widower. You can use this filing status for the two tax years following the year your spouse passed away. It gives you the benefit of joint filing tax tables and a larger standard deduction.

Contact the Social Security Administration—Finally, women who take their husbands' names need to let the Social Security Administration know of the change.

Your Social Security number is key to your tax filings.

Your Social Security number is key to your tax filings. If you do not reconcile your new name and tax ID number, your return could be rejected because of the mismatch. You also could have credits or deductions disallowed or face delayed receipt of your refund.

15

Innocent and injured spouse issues

Most married taxpayers file joint returns. It usually works out well, providing them with a better tax result. But with the benefits come shared responsibilities.

When both a husband and wife sign a return, they agree that each is equally responsible for any tax owed. The legal term is joint and several liability, which essentially means that the IRS can hold either person responsible for all the tax due.

The two signatures also make them liable for tax problems, such as additional tax and any penalties and interest, that arise from errors or omissions on the joint return. It doesn't matter if only one spouse earned all the income or was the person solely responsible for the improper filing.

It also doesn't matter if you're no longer a couple. Even if your marriage doesn't last, your tax liability from those joint filing years does. This is true even when a divorce decree states that a former spouse is responsible for any amounts due on previously filed joint returns.

In some cases, however, you might be able to get off the joint-filing tax hook. The IRS can grant you one of three types of spousal relief—innocent spouse, separation of liability, or equitable relief—if you can show that the questionable tax issues were the fault of your spouse or former spouse.

Innocent spouse—If you meet innocent spouse requirements, you won't have to pay tax, interest, or penalties from that erroneous filing. That payment responsibility will fall solely on your joint return partner.

To qualify as an innocent spouse, you must file a joint return and show

1. The tax on that return was less than it should have been because of unreported income or improper deductions and credits claimed by your spouse or ex-spouse.

2. When you signed the return, you did not know, and had no reason to know, that the amount of tax due on the 1040 was incorrect.

3. Filing circumstance facts that demonstrate it would be unfair to hold you liable for the tax liability.

What the IRS wants to know—To qualify for innocent spouse relief, the IRS requires more than just "I said so" information. The IRS wants specifics on what you did or did not know when you signed the return, as well as detailed data on your income and expenses.

Among the things that the IRS will consider in making its innocent spouse determination are the following:

■ Your educational background and business experience. Did you have the background to realize that the tax filing was not as it should have been?

■ How much you participated in the activity that produced the erroneous item. For example, did you work at your spouse's company for which he or she under-reported income?

■ Whether the filing in question represented a departure from prior return patterns. This could be, for example, the failure to include income from a source that had been reported in previous tax years.

■ Before signing the return, did you ask about items included or left off the form that a reasonable person would question?

Separation of liability—In some cases, the IRS grants separation of liability relief, which protects you from owing the full amount. The understated tax (plus any interest and penalties) is allocated between you and your spouse or ex-spouse.

For this type of relief, you must have filed a joint return and either be divorced or legally separated or lived apart and were estranged from your spouse for 12 months prior to the date you file for relief.

Equitable relief—Equitable relief is granted if you do not meet the innocent spouse or separation of liability requirements.

Whereas the two other types of relief remove or reduce your liability for an understated tax amount—that is, too little tax calculated on your return because of erroneous filing methods—equitable relief can help

> Before signing the return, did you ask about items included or left off the form that a reasonable person would question?

reduce what you might owe in underpaid tax liability. This is the proper tax amount on your joint return, but which has not been fully paid.

Community property considerations—The spousal relief rules are slightly different for married couples who live in a community in one of the nine community property states: Arizona, California, Idaho, Louisiana, Nevada, New Mexico, Texas, Washington, and Wisconsin. In these situations, you still might be able to get relief from liability or equitable relief even if you do not file a joint return.

Determining your relief—Each type of spousal tax relief has slightly different eligibility requirements, but each must be sought by filing Form 8857 within two years from the date the IRS began action against the questionable joint return.

After reviewing the form and other information, the IRS will decide which type of relief, if any, you are eligible to receive. If neither spouse contests the finding, the agency will issue a final determination letter.

Injured spouse relief—Another type of tax relief is sometimes granted to persons the IRS deems as injured spouses. In these cases, the injury is financial, due not necessarily to questionable filing tactics by your spouse, but because other tax considerations that apply only to your husband or wife are causing you money problems, too.

> Another type of tax relief is sometimes granted to persons the IRS deems as injured spouses.

You might be an injured spouse, for example, if you do not receive your portion of a joint tax refund because of collection efforts against your spouse. This typically is the case when a refund is reduced because part of the money is used to pay one spouse's past-due federal or state income taxes, child or spousal support, or other federal debts, such as a student loan. If this is your situation, you can seek your share of the joint refund by filing Form 8379.

16

Tax implications of divorce

Divorce has many consequences, including some potentially dramatic changes to your tax life.

Your filing status likely will go, at least for a while, to single or, depending upon custody arrangements, head of household. Status change alone will affect your tax rates and standard deduction amounts.

Some filing issues could show up before the divorce decree is issued. In many cases, a couple on the outs decides to file separate returns. Talk with not only your divorce attorney, but also your financial and tax adviser before making this change. Couples who file jointly usually enjoy a lower tax liability than do husbands and wives who send in their 1040s separately.

If you are going through a divorce and considering changing your filing method from jointly to separately, run the numbers using each method to see which will be the most advantageous from the tax standpoint.

Keep in mind, too, that the date of your divorce ultimately determines your filing status. If you are divorced on December 30, even though you were married for most of the year, you no longer can file as a married couple. If your divorce is amicable, look at whether staying married a bit longer will give you a better tax result.

Dependent decisions—Marital choices about children are never easy. They get harder during and after a divorce, especially when taxes are involved.

One of the first questions divorcing couples ask is who will claim the children as dependents? The answer could mean a lot tax-wise, since each dependent claim gives the filing parent an exemption amount to help lower his or her tax bill. Some other tax breaks, such as the child dependent care credit, also are limited to the parent who gets to claim the children as dependents.

This tax exemption for a dependent child usually goes to the parent with primary physical custody, regardless of how much child support the other parent pays. Even if the child spends almost as much time with the noncustodial parent, the dependency exemption cannot be split.

As custodial parent, you can agree to let the other parent use the exemption by completing Form 8332 or a similar statement. In friendly divorces, it's not uncommon for ex-spouses to "trade" the child dependency exemption from tax year to tax year, so they can each periodically claim child-related tax breaks. However, before surrendering a child's exemption and associated tax breaks, for one or a series of tax years, talk to your accountant as well as your lawyer.

This tax exemption for a dependent child usually goes to the parent with primary physical custody, regardless of how much child support the other parent pays.

If a divorced couple has several kids, they also could choose to split the dependent exemptions. Again, talk to your tax professional to make sure such a move won't deprive you of tax savings. Usually, it is wiser for the party who benefits the most from the exemptions to claim all of them and consider compensating the other spouse.

Alimony tax costs, benefits—Be careful, though, if that compensation is alimony. A recipient of spousal support must declare that money as income on his or her tax return. The paying spouse, on the other hand, is able to deduct the alimony payments.

Both you and your ex should keep complete and accurate records to document payments and receipts. The IRS can track unreported amounts because for the paying spouse to deduct the support, he or she must include on his or her tax return the former spouse's Social Security number.

Child support, however, is never tax deductible. Neither does it count as income to the parent receiving the payments on behalf of the child or to the child.

Assessing assets—When dividing assets, don't just assess the sentimental or financial value of the property. Take a close look at any tax implications. An asset's tax cost could make a big difference as to whether you want it as part of a property settlement. And an equal dollar division of marital assets could end up costing you substantially more depending upon your financial situation.

For example, you and your ex decide to split a tax-deferred retirement account and a stock fund, each worth $100,000. You take the retirement fund and your former spouse takes the stock account. When you begin taking distributions from the retirement account, you will pay taxes at the ordinary rate. Your spouse, on the other hand, likely has been paying lower rates on that account's capital gains distributions and ultimately can sell the entire fund and face potentially much lower long-term capital gains tax rates.

Don't forget about your home, which is usually a couple's largest asset. If you sell it as a couple, in most cases there is no tax on up to $500,000 in profit. But a single seller only gets half that exclusion amount. Even if you both retain joint ownership, each must live in the property as a principal residence for two of the five years before the sale. Depending upon when you finally dispose of the property, you could lose your maximum joint sale tax break. Selling it as a couple before your divorce is final might be a better tax move.

Other divorce costs—You can't write off legal fees and court costs associated with your divorce, but if you itemize, you might be able to deduct the cost of certain advice in connection with the process. If you received guidance from appraisers, actuaries, and accountants in determining your divorce-related tax bill or help in obtaining alimony, those payments can be claimed as miscellaneous deductions, subject to the 2 percent of adjusted gross income limit, on Schedule A.

Name change details—Finally, if you took your husband's surname during marriage and now are again using your maiden name, let the Social Security Administration know of the change. When you file your return, if your name and tax ID don't match, tax break claims could be denied.

> If you took your husband's surname during marriage and now are again using your maiden name, let the Social Security Administration know of the change.

17

Claiming exemptions and dependents

A family can be a wonderful thing, especially at tax time. By taking care of your children, siblings, or even your parents, you get a break when you file your return. The payoff for your kinship comes when you claim them as dependents.

But first, let's start with the most important member of your tax family: You!

Personal exemptions—Each year, you are allowed to exempt a specific dollar amount (adjusted annually) from your income. There are two types of exemptions: personal exemptions and exemptions for dependents. Each is worth the same amount, but different rules apply to each.

As a single taxpayer, you can claim a personal exemption for yourself. No muss, no fuss. Just check the personal exemption box for yourself on either your 1040 or 1040A. If you're married and filing a joint return, another check box will take care of your spouse's exemption. (Quick note: Exemptions don't specifically appear on Form 1040EZ, but the amount is there, combined with the standard deduction amount.)

Now comes the fun part: claiming your dependents. The IRS recognizes two types of dependents, a child or a relative. For each person who meets the qualification tests under each category, you're allowed a dependent exemption.

Dependent children—This is the most common type of dependent. Still, the IRS demands that your youth tax break meet certain standards, as follows:

- **Relationship**—The youth must be your child, by birth or adoption; step- or foster child; brother, sister, or half sibling; stepbrother or sister; or a descendant of any of them (for instance, a grandchild, niece, or nephew).

- **Age**—The child's birth date is crucial. At the end of the tax year, the child must be younger than 19. If the child is a full-time student, he or she must be younger than 24. However, age is not a factor if the child is permanently and totally disabled.

- **Residency**—The child must have lived with you for more than half of the tax year. There are exceptions for temporary absences, such as a summer-long camp, as well as for children who were born or died during the year and in cases of divorce or separation.

- **Support**—The earnings that matter here are those by the child. The youth cannot provide more than half of his or her own support for the year. This is usually not a problem unless you're the parent of a young *American Idol* winner.

When a child meets all the dependency requirements for more than one person, the two taxpayers can decide which will get the exemption and be able to take other tax child-related breaks. If you can't agree on who will claim the child, the IRS has devised a tie-breaker that takes into account where the child lives for most of the year and the claimant taxpayers' adjusted gross incomes.

Dependent relative—If the person you want to claim as a dependent is a relative but doesn't meet the dependent child tests, he or she can qualify by meeting other rules.

The first one is that the individual can't be the qualifying child of any other taxpayer.

The relative then must live with you for the full tax year. Exceptions are allowed for temporary absences. Children of divorced or separated parents also get special consideration. For example, a child's mother could agree to allow the father to claim the child as a dependent even though the youngster splits time between each parent's home.

If the relative didn't live with you for the requisite time, you still can claim him or her if the person is related to you in a variety of ways. These include the relationships covered by the qualifying child rules, as well as a person who is your parent or stepparent, aunt or uncle, or even in-laws.

> If the person you want to claim as a dependent is a relative but doesn't meet the dependent child tests, he or she can qualify by meeting other rules.

You don't have to worry about your qualifying relative's birthday. Unlike a qualifying child, a dependent here can be any age.

But your relative's earnings do matter. If the relative whom you claim has income, it must be less than the personal exemption amount for the tax year. More earnings are allowed if the relative is disabled and has income from a sheltered workshop.

Finally, you must provide more than half of the relative's total support for the year. Again, exceptions exist, most commonly for children of divorced or separated parents or when multiple support agreements are in effect.

And here's a warning for any dependent you can claim: The person who is eligible to be claimed as a dependent on your return cannot claim a personal exemption on his or her return. For example, you can claim your nephew, who is away at college, as a dependent. He makes some extra cash tutoring fellow students, so he files a return based on those earnings. But since he can be claimed as your dependent, your nephew cannot claim his own personal exemption on his tax return. He's still out of luck even if you choose not to claim him on your return. The mere fact that you could prevents him from taking his personal exemption.

> The person who is eligible to be claimed as a dependent on your return cannot claim a personal exemption on his or her return.

Individuals who cannot be claimed—Even if your prospective dependent meets the qualifying tests, he or she could be disqualified because of some other factors.

You cannot claim any dependents if you, or your spouse when filing jointly, could be claimed as a dependent by another taxpayer. For example, you and your child live with your parents, and they could claim you as a dependent. In this case, you would not be allowed to claim your child on your own tax return.

Citizenship also is a factor. A dependent must be a U.S. citizen, resident alien, or national, or a resident of Canada or Mexico, for some of the tax year. Exceptions are allowed for adopted children.

TRUTH

18

Adoption assistance

Did you add to your growing family via adoption? Then your Uncle Sam wants to help defray some of your costs.

A tax credit is available for qualifying adoption expenses. A credit is more valuable than a tax break. Whereas a deduction reduces your taxable income before you figure your tax, a credit reduces your actual tax due amount. If you are in the 25 percent tax bracket, a $1,000 deduction would produce a tax benefit of $250, but a credit of $1,000 produces a tax benefit of $1,000. Thus, depending upon how much you owe, a credit could zero out your tax bill.

In addition to the adoption tax credit, you may be able to exclude from your income certain expenses that were reimbursed to you by your employer. Known as the *adoption income exclusion*, the money your employer provides to help you add to your family is income tax-free. To qualify for that nontaxable status, the reimbursement must be part of a qualified adoption assistance program; that is, a company fringe benefit available to all employees. When you receive such benefits, they will be reported as nontaxable benefits on your annual W-2 income statement.

You can claim both a tax credit and the income exclusion for the same adoption; just make sure you don't use the same expense for both.

The credit and exclusion amounts for qualifying adoption expenses are adjusted annually for inflation. If you are able to take both the credit and the exclusion, this dollar amount applies separately to each. For example, say the tax-year dollar limit is $10,000 and you incurred eligible adoption expenses of $9,000. Your employer also paid $4,000 in other qualifying costs. You then might be able to claim a $9,000 credit and exclude $4,000 from your income.

However, if you make over a certain threshold amount, which also is inflation adjusted, the adoption tax benefits begin to phase out and could ultimately be eliminated.

> You can claim both a tax credit and the income exclusion for the same adoption; just make sure you don't use the same expense for both.

Precisely how much adoption helps you get from the IRS in a particular tax year also depends on when you paid the expenses, when the adoption was finalized, the nationality of your new child, and, in some cases, your filing status.

Qualifying child—The key consideration in applying for adoption tax breaks is that your new family member meets certain IRS requirements.

Generally, the child must be age 17 or younger. However, he or she can be any age if he or she is physically or mentally disabled. Under certain circumstances, your qualified adoption expenses may be increased when you adopt a special needs child.

Qualifying expenses—The same types of expenses are allowed in calculating the credit and the exclusion. They include reasonable and necessary adoption fees, court costs, attorney fees, and travel expenses, including meal and lodging costs. Other expenses directly related to and for which the principal purpose is the adoption a child also can be counted.

Again, don't count the same expenses for both tax benefits. If your workplace benefit covers your travel costs, you cannot use that amount toward the credit.

Exactly when you can claim these expenses depends not only on the timing of expenses, but also the finalization of the adoption and whether your child is a U.S. citizen or resident alien. In these cases, some costs are claimed in the year they are paid, others must wait until the next year, and others until the adoption is final. Because of the inability to claim some expenses in the year they are made, by the time you are able to claim them, you may have expenses that are greater than the credit amount. In this case, you carry forward the unused amounts for five years or until you use the full credit, whichever comes first.

Details on claim timing can be found in the instructions for Form 8839, which you must file with your tax return.

> Exactly when you can claim these expenses depends not only on the timing of expenses, but also the finalization of the adoption and whether your child is a U.S. citizen or resident alien.

Claiming the credit or exclusion is a bit more restrictive, but simpler, if your child is not a U.S. citizen. In this case, you cannot claim any costs until the year the adoption is final. After that, any subsequent adoption-related expenses can be claimed the year they are paid.

Other considerations—You must file the long Form 1040 or, if you are a nonresident alien, Form 1040NR. A nonresident alien is a person who is not a U.S. citizen and lives outside the country but who has taxable business activities in the United States.

The adoption tax break amount is per child, not per year. That means you are limited to the credit or exclusion amount, regardless of how long it takes or how expensive it is to complete the adoption of your child.

If you adopted a child with special needs, you are eligible to claim the full adoption credit in the year the adoption was final, even if your qualified adoption expenses were less than that amount. To be characterized as special needs, the child must be a U.S. citizen or resident.

Payments to or expenses for a surrogate mother are not eligible for adoption tax credit or exclusion purposes. Neither can you claim the credit for costs of adopting your spouse's child.

If your adoption effort of a U.S. child was unsuccessful, you still can claim eligible expenses incurred during the process. If your adoption attempt was in another country but fell through, you cannot claim those expenses. You must complete a foreign adoption before you can claim the adoption credit.

Payments to or expenses for a surrogate mother are not eligible for adoption tax credit or exclusion purposes.

If you are married, you generally must file a joint return to take the adoption credit or exclusion. You can file as married filing separately, but you then must meet special requirements, such as living apart from your spouse for the last six months of the tax year and solely providing more than half the cost of running the household in which the child lived for more than six months.

TRUTH

19

Child and additional child tax credits

A growing family offers many challenges. Your Uncle Sam wants to help. If you have a child, he'll give you get a tax credit.

Okay. It's not *that* easy. But the process of claiming the Child Tax Credit is relatively painless for many parents of young children.

This tax break's name tells you why it's so beneficial: It's a credit. That means the amount is subtracted directly from any tax you owe, potentially wiping out your tax liability. Currently, it's worth $1,000 per child.

Some parents also are able to claim the Additional Child Tax Credit. If you're eligible for this tax break, it could net you a tax refund.

Credit history—The credit first appeared as the centerpiece of the Taxpayer Relief Act of 1997. Known originally as the Per Child Tax Credit, it was designed to help families deal with the added costs of a larger family by, in many cases, providing them with a tax refund.

It was not the first time that tax credits appeared in the U.S. tax code, but the Per Child Tax Credit signaled a new trend in federal tax policy. Previously, most tax relief had come as lowered rates or increased deductions or exemptions. But once the 1997 tax act paved the way, credits began to regularly show up in tax legislation.

Claiming credit for your kids—For most people, claiming the credit is a piece of cake. You have a kid. The kid has a Social Security number. The kid is younger than age 17 at the end of the tax year. The kid lived with you for more than six months during the tax year. The kid enables you to cut $1,000 off your tax bill.

Of course, even a tax break that's relatively simple is not without a few rules. The main one is that your child be what the IRS calls a qualifying child. That means, he or she

Some parents also are able to claim the Additional Child Tax Credit. If you're eligible for this tax break, it could net you a tax refund.

1. Is a citizen, resident, or national of the United States.
2. Is younger than 17 at the end of the calendar year.

3. Lives with you in your home for more than half the tax year. There are exceptions for parents who are divorced, separated, or living apart. Temporary absences when the child is away from home for school, vacation, medical care, military service, or even in a juvenile detention facility also count as time lived with you for credit purposes.

If your family doesn't follow the traditional June and Ward Cleaver prototype, don't worry.

4. Is not the qualifying child of another taxpayer.

5. Is your son or daughter, either by birth or adoption.

If your family doesn't follow the traditional June and Ward Cleaver prototype, don't worry. For Child Tax Credit purposes, a child also qualifies if he or she is a stepchild or a sibling, either by birth or marriage. The youth also can be a descendant of any of these relatives, such as a grandchild or niece or nephew. A foster child formally placed in your care also qualifies.

Although tax law allows leeway in the relationship of the eligible child, it is firm in its demand that a qualifying child must meet all five conditions: relationship, citizenship, support, age, and residency.

Money matters, too—Income limits could cause your Child Tax Credit amount to be phased out. The amounts vary by filing status and are adjusted annually for inflation.

The amounts are listed in the instructions for Form 1040 or Form 1040A, the two forms that allow claiming of the Child Tax Credit. (Form 1040EZ is for taxpayers without any dependents.) If you make more than the allowed amount, you'll need to use one of the worksheets in IRS Publication 972.

You'll also need to use this publication if you claimed certain tax credits, such as the retirement savings contribution credit or adoption tax credit. The full list of applicable credits and how they might affect your claiming of the Child Tax Credit can be found in Publication 972.

Additional Child Tax Credit—Although the Child Tax Credit is used annually by million of taxpayers to reduce their IRS bills, it only goes so far. It is a nonrefundable credit. That means you can use it to help get your tax bill to zero, but it won't get you a refund.

However, you might be able to get some of that money by claiming the Additional Child Tax Credit. This is a refundable credit, which, as the description indicates, could allow you to get a refund from the IRS once your tax liability is satisfied.

Forms to fill out—You'll use worksheets found in your 1040 or 1040A instructions (or tax software) to compute your Child Tax Credit and enter your allowable amount directly on your tax return.

Some parents also might need to complete Form 8901 to claim the credit. This is necessary if the child you are attempting to claim in connection with the credit is not, according to tax rules, your dependent. This could be the case in a couple of instances:

1. You, or your spouse if you're married and filing jointly, can be claimed as a dependent by someone else. For instance, you, your spouse, and your child are living with your parents, and your parents claim you as a dependent on their own return. Because you are a dependent, you cannot claim your child as a dependent.

2. Your child is married and files a joint tax return with his or her spouse. In this situation, the tax law does not consider the married child your dependent.

If either circumstance applies to you, file Form 8901 to claim the credit in connection with your nondependent child.

As for claiming the Additional Child Tax Credit, most parents will complete Form 8812. If you are eligible for this added tax break, you'll be instructed to use the form when you complete your basic Child Tax Credit worksheet.

Finally, make sure you have Social Security numbers for the children you use to claim these child tax credits. Without them, the IRS will deny your tax break, and you don't want all your work to be for naught because of nine little numbers.

20

Tax help in caring for your kids (and others)

The costs of raising a child are innumerable, but the tax code offers some help for working parents.

When you file your annual return, you might be able to claim the Child and Dependent Care Credit to help offset some daycare costs.

Child care assistance from your employer, typically as a benefit that is excluded from your income, also provides tax savings.

Child care credit—The child care tax credit is designed for working taxpayers, so if you paid someone to look after your child while you were on the job, you've met the credit's first requirement.

If you're married, both you and your spouse must work. The dual-employment requirement is waived if the nonworking spouse was a full-time student. You're also eligible if you needed child care to enable you to look for work.

Next, the child for whom you claim the credit must be your dependent. More importantly, he or she had to be younger than age 13 when the care was provided.

Qualifying care and caregivers—As long as you pay for the child care, most types qualify, from a daycare center to a church program to a neighbor to day camp during school vacations.

Don't try, however, to count a child's tuition costs. If a facility's primary purpose is educational, you cannot consider it child care. Some classes by a caregiver are allowed as long as they are merely add-ons to the primary purpose of caring for the child.

The care also can be in your home. Remember, though, that if you have a nanny or other live-in help, you may have to pay household employer taxes.

Care by most relatives is allowed as long as you pay for the service. Your spouse, however, cannot take care of the kids; remember, this credit is for working individuals. Neither can you claim the credit

As long as you pay for the child care, most types qualify, from a daycare center to a church program to a neighbor to day camp during school vacations.

if you hire one of your children age 18 or younger to care for their siblings.

Other dependents, too—Although most taxpayers who take advantage of this credit do so in connection with their kids, it's also available when you pay for care of other dependents, such as an aging parent who moves in with you.

The person needing the care so you can go to your job can be the following:

1. Your dependent of any age if that person is physically or mentally unable to care for himself or herself.

2. Your spouse if he or she is unable, mentally or physically, to provide self-care.

In these cases, the person must live with you at your primary home for more than half the year.

Credit benefits, within limits—Because this tax break is a credit, the amount for which you qualify will be subtracted directly from any tax you owe, potentially wiping out your tax liability. For example, if you owe $1,000 and qualify for a $500 child care credit, your tax bill is halved.

Exactly how large your credit will be depends on several factors. The number of children being cared for determines how much of your total costs you can apply toward the credit. Currently, you can count $3,000 of the care expenses you paid during the tax year for one person's care, or $6,000 for care of two or more dependents.

Those amounts, however, are not your credit amount. Using Form 2441, you must calculate just how much of your expenses will convert to the credit. Your actual credit is limited to a percentage, ranging from 20 percent to 35 percent of your care dollars, with the largest percentage allowed to lower-earning taxpayers.

Other claim criteria—There are a few other details to note in connection with the child care credit.

Special rules regarding who may claim the credit apply in the case of divorced or separated parents. Generally, the parent with full legal custody of the child takes the credit.

If you are married, you must file a joint return to claim the credit. You also can take it if you file as a qualifying widow or widower, head of household, or single taxpayer.

Get all necessary Social Security numbers. In addition to the tax IDs of the children who received care, you must report on Form 2441 the tax identification number (and name and address) of the care provider; that's the Social Security number of an individual caregiver or, if it's a care facility, the business' employer identification number (EIN). If the care provider is a tax-exempt group, such as a church, you only have to report its name and address. Although technically tax IDs are required, the IRS may allow your credit without the caregiver's number if you can demonstrate you made a good faith effort to get and provide the required information.

Remember, too, that the credit is nonrefundable. It can only take your tax bill to zero, but you'll lose any excess credit amount.

Workplace child care assistance—Some employers offer workers help in caring for their kids. This company benefit takes many forms: direct payment of child care services on behalf of employees, company-provided daycare, or a dependent care spending account. With the spending account option, money is deducted from your paycheck before payroll taxes are withheld, thereby reducing your taxable income. The account money then is used to pay eligible care costs.

The maximum you can put in a workplace child care savings account is $5,000 per family. If you and your spouse each has a care account at work, your combined contributions to both can't exceed $5,000.

Also be careful in coordinating your workplace child care assistance with the tax credit. The IRS frowns on double-dipping, so any untaxed child care help from your employer will reduce the amount of the credit expenses you can claim. For example, you use your spending account to pay $1,000 of your child's daycare; that means you can only use $2,000, not the maximum $3,000 expenses allowed, to figure your child care tax credit amount.

TRUTH

21

Tax-favored college savings options

Congratulations on your new baby! Have you started saving for college yet?

It's not too early. Children do grow up quickly, and higher education costs go up even faster. The good news is that you have several tax-advantaged ways to come up with college cash.

529 plans—529 plans get their name from the Internal Revenue Code section under which they were created. These plans are the overwhelming favorite of families and financial planners alike. Your contributions to a 529 plan are not deductible on your federal return, but the money invested in the plan accumulates tax-free. Even better, when you withdraw account funds to pay for qualified education costs, those distributions are not taxed.

Another appealing aspect of 529s is that they are set up by an adult who names the child as the beneficiary. Anyone can contribute to a 529 plan, such as the beneficiary child's grandparents. Because the money is not in the youth's name, it won't hurt on college financial aid applications. If you want to make sure that parental ownership of the account also doesn't cause any financial aid problems, consider letting another relative (those doting grandparents, perhaps?) set up the plan.

529 plans are administered by states, and every state now has at least one. You don't, however, have to limit yourself to your state's options. You can establish an account with any 529 program. But you might get additional tax advantages, such as a deduction on your state return, by establishing a plan in your home state.

You also can change the beneficiary on the plan if the child for whom it was established decides against college or completes his or her education without using all the money in the plan. Simply roll over plan funds without any tax penalty to a 529 for an immediate family member.

> Your contributions to a 529 plan are not deductible on your federal return, but the money invested in the plan accumulates tax-free.

Coverdell Education Savings Account—Coverdell Education Savings Accounts (ESAs) were once known as education IRAs because the accounts operate much the same way. When the education accounts were expanded in 2002, they were renamed in honor of the late U.S. Senator Paul Coverdell of Georgia.

Coverdell contributions aren't tax-deductible, but they and subsequent earnings can be withdrawn tax-free as long as they are used to pay eligible schooling costs.

Like 529 plans, Coverdell ESAs are established by an adult with the child as the beneficiary. Also like 529s, anyone can contribute to the account, with the annual contribution deadline being the tax year's April filing deadline.

Most financial institutions can serve as home to a Coverdell account. There are, however, some restrictions. Only $2,000 a year is allowed from all contributors, not $2,000 from each. Also, if you make a lot of money, you can't contribute.

On the other hand, Coverdell spending rules are more flexible. Whereas most tax-favored education accounts money must be used for higher education costs, Coverdell money can help pay educational expenses from kindergarten to college, such as a junior high student's new computer.

And as with a 529 plan, if your child doesn't use all the Coverdell money, it can be rolled over to a plan for another family member.

Educational tax credits—Tax credit amounts are subtracted directly from any tax you owe, usually making them a better tax break than deductions, which reduce your taxable income amount. When it comes to education, the tax code offers two popular tax credits.

The Hope Credit helps pay for up to $1,650 in expenses for a freshman or sophomore college student. The credit is per child, so if your son and daughter are in their first two years at State U., then you can claim this credit for each child's eligible expenses. It also can be used for community college or vocational school costs.

The Lifetime Learning Credit is more expansive. This tax break can be used by any student at any level—undergraduate, graduate, or even course work to improve job skills—and the student doesn't have to be enrolled fulltime. The Lifetime Credit is 20 percent of up to $10,000 in educational expenses, meaning you could get a possible $2,000 credit. Also note that the $10,000 limit applies to all educational expenses, not per student. So, if you have several kids in college and their total expenses are more than $10,000, the amount in excess of that won't count toward the Lifetime Credit.

Tuition and fees deduction—This tax break is an above-the-line deduction that can be claimed regardless of whether you claim the standard deduction or itemize. It's found on both Form 1040 and 1040A and could reduce your taxable income by as much as $4,000. This deduction technically is temporary, but for the last few years, Congress has renewed the tax break.

Although its above-the-line status makes this tax break more available, it does have some limits. If you make over a certain amount, your deduction amount is reduced. If you claim one of the education tax credits, you cannot use this deduction for other expenses by the same student in the same year.

You can, however, take the tuition and fees deduction, as well as distributions from Coverdell ESAs and 529 plans, as long as you paid for different educational expenses with the various funds.

> You can take the tuition and fees deduction, as well as distributions from Coverdell ESAs and 529 plans, as long as you paid for different educational expenses with the various funds.

Student loan interest deduction—This is another above-the-line deduction that enables you to deduct up to $2,500 in student loan interest. It, too, is phased out for higher-income taxpayers. If you're married, you must file a joint return to take this deduction.

Savings bonds—When you cash in U.S. savings bonds, you must pay tax on the deferred interest that the bonds earned. But if you use the bonds to pay for educational expenses, the interest could be tax-free.

TRUTH

22

When a child has to file

A summer or part-time job is a great experience for a youngster. The young worker learns responsibility and pockets a bit of spending money to boot. But with those paychecks come possible tax consequences.

Basically, there is no age limit, high or low, that establishes whether you have to file. Age is a factor, but the primary determinants are the amount and type of income received. The IRS characterizes income in three ways:

- Earned income, which comes from work, such as wages, salary, or tips. This type of income is reported on Form W-2, detailing the amount earned and any taxes that might have been withheld. Earned income also could be from self-employment. For a young worker, self-employment income could come from babysitting or mowing neighborhood lawns.

- Unearned income comes from investments, usually in the form of interest, dividends, capital gains distributions, or capital gains from the sale of assets. These amounts will be reported on Form 1099-DIV or 1099-INT or similar statements issued by investment companies.

- Gross income, which is a combination of earned and unearned income.

When a young person who is a dependent of another taxpayer has income, the amounts of money in each of the three categories determine whether the youngster has to file a return. Remember, the IRS gets a copy of each W-2 or 1099 form sent to the young earner, so don't ignore your child's potential filing duties.

Wage income—When your dependent youngster has only earned income as an employee, he or she doesn't need to file a return if the total reported on the W-2 is less than the standard deduction for a single filer that tax year. The deduction amount is adjusted each year for inflation. You can find this on Form 1040 and Form 1040A and in both forms' instructions.

Self-employment income—If a young person earns income from self-employment, such as babysitting or lawn mowing, that money is subject to income tax. The youngster can deduct eligible expenses, such as lawn equipment or gasoline for the mower, to get to a lower taxable earnings amount. The self-employment income and expenses are reported by the young taxpayer on Schedule C or C-EZ and filed with Form 1040.

Even if a young person's self-employment income is not enough to meet the standard deduction amount to require filing, the youth might have to file to pay self-employment tax. This is required when anyone has self-employment net earnings of more than $400. The self-employment tax, filed on Schedule SE, pays for Social Security and Medicare benefits; it is the self-employed person's version of FICA taxes that are withheld from salaried or wage jobs. The good news about self-employment taxes is that half of the amount can be deducted on Form 1040.

One exception to self-employment for young entrepreneurs is when they are newspaper carriers or vendors younger than 18. In this case, the youth's earnings are not subject to self-employment tax.

Unearned income—If your dependent child has only unearned income, whether he or she has to file depends solely on how much was received in the tax year.

Unearned income includes taxable interest, dividends, capital gains (including capital gain distributions), and distributions from trusts. The amounts generally are reported on various 1099 forms or substitute forms provided by the account manager.

The amount necessary to trigger a filing requirement, known as the kiddie tax, is adjusted periodically to reflect inflation. You'll find the amount in the Form 1040 and Form 1040A instructions or on www. IRS.gov.

When the child's investment earnings exceed the year's amount, then the youth must file a return. In these cases, the parent also has the option to include the child's unearned income on the adult's tax return so that the child doesn't have to file a return. However, before you decide to count your child's earnings as your income, talk with your tax adviser to make sure you understand what effect your child's added income might mean to your tax liability.

> The amount necessary to trigger a filing requirement is adjusted periodically to reflect inflation.

89

Gross income—When a youngster collects both unearned income and wages, the IRS considers the youth's gross income in determining whether a return must be filed. The calculation gets a bit more complicated, and the exact trigger amounts change annually. You can find the applicable figures in the individual tax return instructions.

> If taxes were withheld from the young worker's wages and he or she is due a refund, the only way to get the money back is to file a 1040.

Other potentially taxable income—Students who receive a scholarship or fellowship may find that all or part of such educational aid is taxable.

Generally, the entire amount is taxable if you are not working toward a degree. If you are a candidate for a degree, you generally can exclude from income that part of the grant that is used to pay tuition and fees, or for books, supplies, and equipment.

Any of the scholarship or fellowship money that goes toward room and board must be counted as taxable income.

Claim a refund—Even when your youngster doesn't expressly have to file a return, it might be worthwhile to do so. If taxes were withheld from the young worker's wages and he or she is due a refund, the only way to get the money back is to file a 1040.

TRUTH

23

Taking tax-smart care of a parent

Millions of Americans care for an elderly relative, usually a parent. As the baby boomers age, this number will keep growing.

If you're one of these caregivers, or expect to soon join their ranks, make sure you get some help from the tax code.

If your elderly parent qualifies as your dependent, you'll be able to claim another exemption on your return. This will help lower your taxable income amount. You also might be able to deduct some of your parent's medical expenses or even claim the dependent care credit.

First, however, you must make sure that the IRS will accept your mom or dad as a qualifying relative.

Dependent relative requirements—If you have children of your own, you already know that the tax code demands your dependents meet certain tests. But the standards for a qualifying child and a qualifying relative are not quite the same.

There are four criteria that a person must meet before he or she is considered an IRS-approved qualifying relative.

The first two shouldn't be a problem:

1. The person cannot be your qualifying child or the qualifying child of another taxpayer.

2. The person must be related to you. A variety of relationships count, and yes, parents (and stepparents) are on the list.

The next two requirements, however, could be more difficult to meet. Both are concerned with money.

Parental income issues—First, your parent's earnings must be less than the personal exemption amount for the tax year. You'll find the amount for each tax year on the current 1040 and 1040A forms.

Your parent's income amount includes both earned income—for example, a part-time job your parent may have—as well as unearned money, such as distributions from investments. Social Security benefits don't count, but if your folks saved for their retirement, their successful financial planning could pose problems for you now as you try to claim them as dependents.

Supporting your folks—Then your money is taken into account.

You must provide more than half of your parent's total support. This includes food, housing, medical care, transportation, recreation, and other necessities. If you've made it over the parental income hurdle, you might think you're okay here, too. But under this dependent test, Social Security benefits count. So do nontaxable pensions, tax-exempt interest, savings, welfare benefits, nontaxable life insurance proceeds, and even borrowed money.

To determine whether you provided more than half of your parent's total support, you must compare the amount you contributed to mom's or dad's support with the entire amount of support he or she received from all sources, including you.

> To determine whether you provided more than half of your parent's total support, you must compare the amount you contributed to mom's or dad's support with the entire amount of support he or she received from all sources.

For example, your mom had earned income of $600, Social Security benefits of $3,000, and tax-exempt interest of $400, all of which she uses for her support. You pitched in $2,500 toward her support during the year. You cannot claim an exemption for her.

Although your $2,500 contribution to mom's living expenses is more than half of her $4,000 total income, her total support amount is $6,500 thanks to your added money. And your $2,500 contribution is not more than half of that total amount.

The IRS provides a worksheet in Publication 501 to help you make sure you meet the support test.

Moving your parent into your home or other property you own could help you meet this requirement. The IRS considers that you provide support equal to the fair rental value of the room, apartment, house, or other shelter you made available to your parent.

But your parent or parents don't have to live with you for housing support to be a factor. If mom and dad are able to remain in their own home, or have moved to an assisted living facility, 93 any amounts you pay toward those residential arrangements count as support that can be used to meet this IRS requirement.

Shared support—Many families combine resources to take care of aging parents. In these cases, you and your siblings must decide which of you can claim mom or dad as a dependent.

You will have to do some calculations. If none of you is providing the requisite 51 percent or more of support, but all of your combined financial contributions do amount to more than half of your parent's support, then any sibling who provides more than 10 percent can claim the parent as a dependent.

Because only one of you can claim your parent in a tax year, you must decide who gets the exemption. You can let the sibling who gets the most tax benefit have the exemption, or you can agree to rotate the exemption among yourselves. Check out IRS Form 2120, Multiple Support Declaration.

Medical costs—Once mom or dad meet the IRS dependency tests, you can count any parental medical costs you pay toward Schedule A itemized medical deductions. Because medical costs must exceed 7.5 percent of your adjusted gross income before you can claim them, adding your parent's medical bills might help you meet this threshold.

And even if your parent doesn't qualify as a dependent for exemption purposes because he or she earned too much, if mom or dad meet the other tests, you can count your parent as a dependent for medical deduction purposes.

Dependent care credit—If your parent lives with you and requires constant care, the cost of hiring someone to provide nursing so that you can go to work could qualify you for the dependent care credit. Only the first $3,000 you spend for such care counts, and then only a percentage of that dollar amount can be claimed. But because it is a credit, whatever amount that you qualify for is subtracted directly from any tax you owe.

> Because medical costs must exceed 7.5 percent of your adjusted gross income before you can claim them, adding your parent's medical bills might help you meet this threshold.

TRUTH

24

Getting your withholding right

"*U*nquestionably, there is progress.
The average American now pays out
twice as much in taxes as he formerly
got in wages. "

—H.L. Mencken, author

A lot of folks intentionally have too much tax withheld from their paychecks. They consider it an automatic savings account that pays off with a refund when they file their returns.

The Internal Revenue Service likes this process, too, since the agency gets an interest-free loan from these overwithholding advocates.

Withholding is a crucial component of the U.S. tax system, which operates on a pay-as-you-earn arrangement. Essentially, the IRS wants the appropriate amount of taxes on your money as soon as or shortly after you get it.

But overwithholding isn't the best way to meet your tax obligations. Not only are you giving up use of your hard-earned dollars throughout the year, but you also have to wait to get that money back. Sometimes that payback can be quite slow.

It's not a good idea to underwithhold, either. Sure, having too few taxes taken out of your check gives you more spending money throughout the year, but then you must come up with a lump payment by April 15. And if you underwithhold by a large amount, penalty and interest charges could be tacked onto your tax bill.

The smartest tax strategy is to have your payroll withholding be as close as possible to your eventual tax liability. Putting the proper withholding into effect is easy. You simply give your employer a new W-4.

But figuring out if you're under- or overwithholding, and just how to correct it, is a little trickier.

You're having too much withheld if...—The most obvious signal that you're having too much taken out of your paycheck is that you got a big refund last tax year. If your income, adjustments, deductions, and credits will remain about the same this year, you need to reexamine your withholding.

> The smartest tax strategy is to have your payroll withholding be as close as possible to your eventual tax liability.

Of course, most of the time, life doesn't continue exactly as it did before. So, you also need to be careful about overwithholding if your income will remain about the same, but your adjustments and deductions will increase significantly. For example, you bought a house and will be deducting mortgage interest and property tax payments on your upcoming return. Accounting for those deductions will get you more money in your paycheck to buy furniture for the new place. New or additional tax credits you'll claim on your 1040 also could affect your tax bill, meaning you don't want to have too much withheld.

To reduce the amount of payroll taxes taken out of your check, give your employer a W-4 listing more withholding allowances.

You're having too little withheld if...—Did you take a second job this year? It's possible, depending on how much you make at both workplaces, that your added income will mean a larger tax bill when you file. Underwithholding also could be a problem if your spouse works and you didn't coordinate your withholding allowances. Account for all these jobs in your W-4.

If you have other income that is not taxed when you receive it, you're probably not paying enough tax throughout the year. This money typically comes in as capital gains, rental income, interest, or dividends. The responsibility for making sure the appropriate amount of tax is paid falls to you, typically via estimated tax payments. But you also can increase your withholding at work to cover the added income's taxes.

Other taxes, such as self-employment tax due in connection with a venture you operate on weekends or household employment taxes you pay in connection with your child's nanny, also could mean you're not having enough taken out of your paychecks.

In underwithholding situations, you need to give your payroll office a new W-4 with fewer allowances. You also can ask your employer to withhold a specific dollar amount from your check each payday.

Periodically check your withholding—It's a good idea to check your withholding throughout the year. And definitely reassess your W-4 allowances when there are personal or financial changes in your life. These include the following:

- Lifestyle changes, such as marriage, divorce, birth or adoption of a child, or purchase of a new home.

- Changes to your wages, such as when you or your spouse start or stop working or start or stop a second job.

- Increases or reductions in income not subject to withholding, such as interest income, dividends, capital gains, self-employment earnings, or IRA distributions.

- Increases or reductions in adjustments to income, such as student loan interest or alimony payments.

- Changes, up or down, in itemized deductions or tax credits, such as medical expenses, state income, sales or property taxes, charitable donations, education credits, or child tax credits.

The earlier in the year you check your withholding, the easier it is to have the right amount of tax withheld.

Calculating the correct withholding amount—Form W-4 has several worksheets to help you figure out your proper withholding amount. They include the Personal Allowances worksheet, the Deductions and Adjustments worksheet, and the Two-Earners/Multiple Jobs worksheet.

Many tax software programs also can help you calculate your appropriate withholding amount. Some tax software programs even prompt you to refigure your withholding if, when you used the software to complete your tax return, you ended up owing a lot or got a sizeable refund.

You also can use the IRS' own online tool to come up with your correct W-4 information. Simply go to www.IRS.gov and type "withholding calculator" into the search box at the top right of the web page.

When you know the correct number of allowances to claim and have given that data to your employer via a new W-4, your boss has about a month to process the changes. However, most workplaces turn around the payroll changes much more quickly. Just keep an eye on your paycheck to make sure that your new, and tax-smart, withholding amounts are eventually reflected in your paycheck.

TRUTH

25

Tax-favored employer-provided benefits

Happy employees are more productive employees. That's why companies offer benefits. The bonus for workers is that many benefit programs also offer tax savings.

Tax code provisions play a major role in workplace retirement plans. You also might be able to reduce your tax bill while staying healthy, caring for your kids, adding to your family, or finally getting your graduate degree. Some workplaces even provide tax-advantaged ways to get you into the office.

The key to maximizing these benefits is knowing just what your company offers and which ones fit your circumstances. Here are some programs to ask your human resources office about.

Retirement accounts— Companies used to bear most of the responsibility for employee pension plans. But now, 401(k) plans, named after the tax code section that created them, are the primary way for workers to build their retirement nest eggs.

Firms typically offer a variety of investment choices, and you have a percentage of your paycheck directly deposited into the 401(k) plan option of your choice. The money goes into the account before payroll taxes are withheld, lowering your taxable income.

Many companies also match a percentage of your contributions. Earning on that company money and your own payroll deposits grow tax-deferred.

Some companies also offer Roth 401(k) plans. These plans work the same way traditional 401(k) plans do, but Roth payroll contributions are made after taxes are withheld. The appeal of this method is that your eventual Roth 401(k) distributions are tax-free.

Healthcare options—Medical care tops almost every employee's list of must-have workplace benefits. The tax code, however, has changed the way this popular benefit is provided.

Most workplace medical coverage nowadays is part of a Section 125 plan, more commonly known as a cafeteria plan. Your boss offers you a selection of benefits, and you choose the ones that meet your personal and family needs.

In most cases, you pay your portion of health insurance premiums with pretax dollars that are taken out via payroll deductions. Another popular tax-advantaged cafeteria plan option is a flexible spending account (FSA). Again, the money is deducted from your paycheck before taxes.

You then use medical FSA money to pay for such things as insurance copayments, for both doctor office visits and prescriptions, as well as for treatments that aren't covered by your insurance, such as chiropractic sessions or vision care. Even over-the-counter medications can be paid for with medical FSA money.

Kiddie care—Another popular FSA can help you pay some child care expenses. Up to $5,000 can be put, pretax, into a dependent care FSA to pay daycare costs.

If both you and your spouse have a dependent care account at your respective offices, note that the $5,000 limit is per family, not per employee or child. Run the numbers to determine which of you benefits the most from putting the maximum in a child care FSA.

Although these accounts typically are used by parents facing child care expenses, the money also can go toward costs incurred to care for any other eligible dependent, such as an elderly parent living in your home, who needs looking after while you go to work.

FSA pros, cons—The one downside of flexible spending accounts is the use-it-or-lose-it provision. If you don't spend the money in the accounts by the end of your benefit year, you forfeit any excess cash.

This generally is more of an issue with medical FSA accounts. So, estimate carefully how much you believe you might need in your account during the benefit year. It's usually better to put in too little rather than too much.

Employers do have the option to grant a 2.5-month grace period during which you can use your leftover FSA money, but it's not a requirement. Check with your human resources office about your company's FSA deadlines.

> The one downside of flexible spending accounts is the use-it-or-lose-it provision.

Use of a child care FSA also will limit the amount of the dependent care credit you can claim when you file your tax return.

But an upside of FSAs, in addition to the pretax funding aspect of the accounts, is that you can get to the money when you need it. You can use FSA funds to pay qualifying costs even if you haven't yet built up a sufficient amount in the account. As long as you've set up a payroll deduction schedule that ultimately will give you a certain amount, you can access that money any time.

For example, $250 of each monthly paycheck goes into your medical FSA. In June, your son has a bicycle accident requiring uninsured orthodontia treatment costing $2,500. Although you've put only $1,500 into your FSA (6 months × $250), you can get a disbursement to pay the bill in full because your eventual FSA amount will cover the dentist's total bill.

Commuting costs—Some workplaces help employees pay commuting costs with an FSA-style account known as a qualified transportation benefit, or QTB, account or commuter savings account. These accounts help pay for eligible transit passes, fare cards, or vouchers. If you drive to work instead of taking mass transit, you can use the money to pay parking expenses.

Adoption expenses—Workers who adopt children might be able to expand their family and save on taxes via a company-provided assistance program. In this case, you can exclude from your income certain adoption expenses that were reimbursed to you by your employer. Check with your company about the eligible amount, which is adjusted annually for inflation.

Educational assistance—If you want to further your education, check with your boss. You may receive up to $5,250 in tax-free education benefits from your employer each year. Eligible educational assistance typically includes payments for tuition, fees, books, supplies, and equipment. The payments may be for undergraduate- or graduate-level courses. Even better, the benefit payments are not limited to work-related courses.

> Some workplaces help employees pay commuting costs with an FSA-style account known as a qualified transportation benefit, or QTB, account or commuter savings account.

26

Recouping employee business expenses

Sometimes doing your job means spending your own money. Ideally, you would be reimbursed for your job-related expenditures. But that doesn't always happen. In those cases, you might be able to write off your employee business expenses.

You must itemize—The first requirement in recouping your unreimbursed business expenses is that you itemize your deductions on Schedule A. You'll enter them in the section entitled Job Expenses and Certain Miscellaneous Deductions.

Just itemizing, however, is not enough. All of those costs must be more than 2 percent of your adjusted gross income.

Note also that only the amount in excess of the 2 percent threshold is deductible. For example, your adjusted gross income (AGI) is $50,000. Two percent of that amount is $1,000. You have miscellaneous expenses of $1,200, giving you $200 in deductible expenses.

What you can deduct—The IRS has two standards—ordinary and necessary—that job expenses must meet before your can count them as part of your itemized deductions.

An *ordinary expense* is one that is common and accepted in your trade, business, or profession.

A *necessary expense* is one that is appropriate and helps you do your job. An expense doesn't have to be required by your employer for it to be considered necessary.

You'll see on Schedule A that job travel, union dues, and job education costs are listed as acceptable work-related miscellaneous deductions. Other allowable costs include the following:

■ Tools and supplies used in your work

■ Work clothes and uniforms, and their upkeep costs, for apparel that is required by your employer but that isn't suitable for ordinary, off-the-job wear

■ Protective clothing required for your job, such as hard hats, safety shoes, and glasses or goggles

■ Medical examinations required by an employer

- Professional organization dues

- Legal fees related to doing or keeping your job

- Licenses and regulatory fees, as well as occupational taxes

- Subscriptions to professional journals and trade magazines

Certain education expenses also can be counted if the instruction is required by law or by your employer to maintain or improve your skills and keep your current salary, status, or position.

And although commuting is critical to doing your job, those miles are not deductible. Some other local transportation expenses, however, might be. For example, the cost of going from one workplace to another can be counted. When claiming your unreimbursed work-related travel, as well as any associated entertainment and meal expenses, you'll need to complete Form 2106 or Form 2106-EZ and attach it to your tax return.

What you can't deduct—Although there are many work-related expenses you can claim if you're not reimbursed by your boss, the IRS does draw some lines.

For example, don't try to push the membership dues category. If you belong to a group whose primary purpose is social, not professional, expect the IRS to disallow that expense.

The agency also specifically states that you cannot deduct the following:

> Although commuting is critical to doing your job, those miles are not deductible.

- Political contributions

- Costs of entertaining friends

- Meals eaten during regular or extra work hours

- Legal expenses for personal matters that do not produce taxable income

- Costs of attending a seminar, convention, or similar meeting that is not related to your employment

Writing off a home office, phone—Home offices and associated equipment is a well-known deduction for small businesses. But you also might be able to write off this expense as an employee if you routinely work from home.

As with businesses, the office space in your home must be used regularly and exclusively for work purposes. This can be home office space used to conduct your principal business tasks or as a place to meet or deal with clients or customers in the normal course of your trade or business.

The key requirement to claim home office costs on your Schedule A is that the residential office space be for the convenience of your employer. Just making your job easier doesn't cut it with the IRS.

You can claim a depreciation deduction (filed on Form 4562) for a computer or cell phone that you use in your work as an employee if its use is for the convenience of your employer. Use of the equipment during your regular working hours to conduct your employer's business is generally considered to be for the convenience of your employer.

The equipment also must be required as a condition of your employment. Your employer doesn't have to explicitly require you to use your computer or mobile phone to hang onto your job. What the IRS wants to see is that you cannot properly perform your duties without the equipment.

Document your deductions—Finally, remember that record keeping is critical when it comes to claiming and defending, if the IRS asks, your unreimbursed work expenses.

Remember that record keeping is critical.

Well-organized records will make it easier to prepare your tax return and will help you answer questions if your return is selected for examination, or prepare any response if you are billed for additional tax.

Hang onto to receipts, canceled checks, and other documents that support your deductions. If you use your auto in connection with your job duties, it's a good idea to keep a log of your work-related road trips.

Writing off job-hunting costs

If it's time to find another job, you know how much networking can help. Just make sure you don't overlook some outside assistance that could pay off when you start collecting a paycheck from your new employer: the tax code.

You can deduct many of your job-hunting expenses. That's not that surprising, since it's in the Internal Revenue Service's best interest to have you earning taxable income.

Uncle Sam's tax help, however, does have its limits.

Itemizing required—You must itemize deductions on Schedule A to count your job-hunting expenses.

That task is further limited by a threshold amount you must meet. Your job search costs are considered miscellaneous expenses. As such, they are deductible on when they, and all other allowable expenses in this category, are more than 2 percent of your adjusted gross income.

That means, for example, if your adjusted gross income (AGI) is $30,000, you must have miscellaneous expenses that add up to more than $600. So, if you have $650 in allowable expenses, you can deduct only $50.

The good news is that there are many miscellaneous expenses you can include on this section of Schedule A. In fact, some expenses you incurred at the job you are leaving but for which you weren't reimbursed can be added in to help get you over the 2 percent threshold hurdle.

Don't look too far afield—The other big obstacle in writing off your job search costs is the type of work you're seeking.

You can deduct expenses only if you're looking for another job in the same occupation. If you're an engineer and want to go from Smith Construction to Jones Construction, the IRS will help pay costs incurred to make that office switch.

But if you want to leave Smith Construction and start a new career with Watson's Catering, don't expect any help from Uncle Sam.

The IRS also won't allow your deductions if you took a substantial

> You can deduct expenses only if you're looking for another job in the same occupation.

break between your last job and your search for a new one. Basically, the IRS won't help subsidize your job hunt if, for example, you took a year off to travel or care for your kids.

And sorry new graduates. You can't deduct job search expenses if you're knocking on doors trying to get your first full-time paying gig. Of course, if that first job is not the one of your dreams, start looking again within your profession, and this time take advantage of the tax breaks.

The one bit of good news among all these restrictions is that as long as you haven't taken a sizeable work break and are looking for employment within your current profession, you can write off eligible search costs even if you don't get a new job.

What counts—Now to the important question: What can you write off?

Just about anything counts as a job search expense, starting with your résumé. You can deduct amounts you spend for preparing the document, including fees for professional help in tweaking it to catch an employer's eye. Once it's ready to go, be sure to note the delivery costs; they're deductible, too.

If you get help beyond shaping your résumé or curriculum vitae (C.V.), that's also deductible. This includes employment and outplacement agency fees that help you look for a new job in your present field. Be careful here, however. If your new employer later pays you back for those employment agency fees, you might need to include at least some of that repayment money in your gross income. Essentially, the IRS doesn't want you to get a free deduction based on money that you then, in tax terms, recovered.

Also keep track of the cost of advertising your services, newspapers, and other periodicals you purchased to monitor their help-wanted ads and legal fees paid to an attorney to review an employment contract.

Some travel expenses incurred in your employment search also can be deducted. This includes some food expenses, as well as lodging and, in some instances, transportation to and from another city to look for a job.

Keep in mind that the trip must primarily be to look for a new job. You can't go visit your cousin in Kansas City, drop off a résumé at

No matter what you eventually choose to deduct, it will all be disallowed unless you can show receipts for your expenses.

ABC Corporation, and then deduct your transportation costs. Some personal time, however, is allowed. Just make sure that the amount of time you spend on personal activity is substantially less than the time you spend looking for work.

No matter what you eventually choose to deduct, it will all be disallowed unless you can show receipts (not just a monthly credit card statement) for your expenses, including a mileage log for the car with start/finish odometer readings, date, and purpose of the trip.

Even if you cannot deduct the travel expenses to and from an area, you can deduct the expenses of looking for a new job while in the area. This could be, for example, the cost of a rental car or cab fare to go from the hotel (or your cousin's house) to meet with ABC Corporation's personnel department.

If you use your own car to make job search trips, either out of town or within your current city, keep track of the odometer readings. You can use the standard mileage rate to figure your car expenses. This per-mile rate varies each year, and sometimes within a year, depending on, in large part, current gasoline prices. Check www.IRS.gov for the latest rates.

Have you decided to strike out on your own? The costs of looking into that enterprise also can count as long as your self-employment effort is in the same field as your last job.

Remember, when you become your own boss, the same documentation guidelines apply to those deductions, too.

TRUTH

28

Tax help in paying work-related moving costs

Did you take the proverbial advice to go west? If so, and your travel west, or any direction for that matter, was in connection with a job, the tax code could help you cover your relocation costs.

The tax break for moving expenses is relatively easy to claim. It's right there near the bottom of your Form 1040. The nice thing about its location there is that you don't have to itemize to claim this deduction.

If you do itemize, that's okay, too. You still can take this above-the-line deduction, so called because it's part of a group of tax breaks on the 1040 that appear just above the line where you enter your adjusted gross income.

But because you don't have to itemize, there are no threshold amounts, such as costs related to a percentage of your income, to meet. And you don't have to worry about your deduction being reduced because, in the IRS's eyes, you make too much money.

You will, however, have to fill out another piece of tax paperwork, Form 3903, to claim your moving expenses.

Before you can work through the tax form, though, your move has to pass a couple of other IRS tests. How far you moved and the amount of time you spend on the job once you're there will determine whether you qualify for the moving expenses tax break.

Distance test—Moves that are only short hops usually don't qualify for this deduction. What's too short? The IRS says less than 50 miles. And that distance is directly connected to your previous home and your pre- and post-move jobs.

Basically, your new job must be at least 50 miles further from your old home than was your previous workplace. Here's a sample calculation:

Miles from old home to new workplace:	60
Miles from old home to old workplace:	5
Difference between the two:	55

In this case, you're fine. The location of your new job is 55 miles farther from your previous home than was your prior workplace.

Basically, what the IRS is trying to prevent is folks getting a tax break for moves that primarily eased their commutes or were simply to change neighborhoods instead of required because of a changing job.

And in figuring the mileage, the IRS says to use the shortest of the more commonly traveled routes. In other words, don't take detours just to make sure you meet the 50-mile requirement.

How far you moved and the amount of time you spend on the job once you're there will determine whether you qualify for the moving expenses tax break.

Time test—The next test deals with time on the job. You won't be able to qualify for the moving expenses deduction if your relocation was for a short-term or part-time position.

Rather, the IRS says you must work full-time for at least 39 weeks during the 12 months immediately after your move. That's 75 percent of the time.

If you are self-employed, the time test has two parts. In addition to working the 39 weeks, as do the folks who go into an employer's office, your total self-employment effort must extend into the second year of your move. Officially, you're required to work for at least 78 weeks during the first two years after your move.

The weeks, either as an employee or as your own boss, don't have to be sequential. They don't even have to be with the same employer. But if the IRS asks, you must show that you are indeed working and have met or expect to meet the requite number of weeks of employment.

If you're married, as long as you file a joint return, then only one spouse has to meet the time and distance tests.

And go ahead and claim your moving expenses if the tax-filing deadline arrives before you satisfy the time test. If it so happens that you don't ultimately meet the time requirement, you can file an amended return or add the expenses you deducted to your income the next tax year.

New job is okay—As taxpayers know all too well, the tax laws are, shall we say, sometimes a bit curious. A look at the moving expenses

113

and job-hunting deductions is a good example of work-related write-offs that aren't always applied uniformly.

Job-hunting expenses you incur in looking for your first full-time job aren't deductible. But if that first job requires you to move more than 50 miles, you can deduct the relocations costs.

Members of the armed forces also are granted special exceptions when a move is part of a militarily mandated relocation.

Just which costs count?—The IRS says "reasonable" moving expenses are deductible, and you can include the costs of transporting your household goods and personal items to your new place. You also can write off a portion of your own travel expenses. Special arrangements for pets and autos also are deductible. So are, in some cases, the cost of storing your property after you move.

However, some expenses are specifically excluded. Meals eaten while in transit to your new home are not deductible moving expenses (another provision to file under that "curious" category); neither are house hunting expeditions to your new city. And don't even think about trying to deduct the price of vehicle tags required by your new jurisdiction.

IRS Publication 521, available for downloading at www.IRS.gov, contains an extensive list of deductible and nondeductible expenses.

Employer-provided relocation assistance—When your boss gets involved in your move, that, too, could produce some tax considerations.

If you receive reimbursement from your employer for your moving expenses, how you report the amount depends on what kind of relocation plan your company has established under IRS rules. A company can give you reimbursement amounts that are not included in your taxable income, or it can add the moving-related money to your salary. Ask your employer for details on what method it uses and what records you need to keep in connection with the moving assistance.

And if you are reimbursed for some or all of your moving expenses, don't get greedy and try to double-dip. You're not allowed to deduct moving costs if they are paid by your employer.

TRUTH
29

Self-employment tax considerations

Being your own boss has lots of advantages. It also comes with plenty of responsibilities, including new tax tasks.

Some of your tax duties will cost you, both time and money. Others, however, provide some savings.

Your business tax identity—How you set up your business determines in large part what forms to file, your tax deadlines, and even if the IRS wants a new taxpayer identification number from you.

For example, if you operate you business as a corporation or a partnership, you'll need to obtain an Employer Identification Number (EIN). An EIN also is required if you have employees. You can get an EIN at no cost by calling the IRS's Business and Specialty Tax division at (800) 829-4933 or applying for one online at www.IRS.gov.

If, however, you operate your business as a sole proprietor, you can continue to use your Social Security number in connection with your seff-employment earnings. You simply report the income on your Form 1040 after you calculate the correct amount on Schedule C or C-EZ.

Paying "extra" tax—Now that you work for yourself, one of your major tax considerations is federal self-employment tax. This is a Social Security and Medicare tax similar to the FICA amounts withheld from the pay of most wage earners. If you have net earnings of $400 or more, you must pay self-employment tax by filing Schedule SE with your tax return.

When you were an employee, you paid half of this amount and your company matched the other half. Now, as both employee and employer, you cover the full cost. But the one good thing about paying this tax is that you can deduct half of it on your Form 1040.

> If you operate your business as a sole proprietor, report your earnings on your Form 1040 after calculating the correct amount on Schedule C or C-EZ.

You also need to consider your self-employment tax amount when figuring estimated tax payments. Because you are now earning money that does not have any payroll taxes withheld, it's your responsibility to pay the tax throughout the year yourself by filing estimated tax Form 1040-ES vouchers. These payments generally are due the 15th of April (as a separate filing from your personal return), June, September, and the following January.

Reducing your taxable income—So that your ultimate tax bill, and the estimated tax payments you have to make before then, are as low as possible, you want to reduce your gross self-employment income through deductions.

A look at Schedule C reveals the wide array of expenses that you can claim to lower your self-employment income. Page 1 has two dozen lines for business-related write-offs, such as the following:

- Office supplies, furniture, and certain equipment
- Repairs and maintenance costs
- Legal and professional fees, including professional license costs
- Advertising and promotional expenses
- Subscriptions to trade or professional publications

More detailed write-offs you can claim on Schedule C include the following:

- Equipment depreciation
- Car and truck expenses
- A home office
- Travel, meals, and entertainment expenses

IRS Publication 334 offers details on allowable businesses expenses. It also notes what expenses you cannot deduct.

Special deduction considerations—When it comes to meals and entertainment, you can deduct only 50 percent of these expenses. Don't try to compensate for this percentage reduction by taking clients to the most expense place in town. The IRS says business meal costs can't be lavish or extravagant. Seemingly excessive claims are an auditor's dream.

IRS examiners also look closely at vehicle expenses. A separate section on page 2 of Schedule C asks for details about the auto you used for business purposes.

Home office deductions are more common nowadays. But the IRS still demands plenty of substantiation via Form 8829, which is filed in conjunction with Schedule C.

And health insurance costs, a major expense for self-employed workers, can be deducted, just not on your Schedule C. Instead, any amount you pay for medical coverage for yourself, and your spouse and dependents if this is your family's only health care, can be claimed on your Form 1040.

Retirement plan contributions—Another key self-employment deduction that shows up on the 1040 instead of Schedule C is money you put into a qualified retirement plan. The benefits of these retirement plans are twofold. You save for the eventual day when you can quit working, and you get an immediate tax deduction for your contributions.

As more people have joined the self-employment ranks, the types of retirement plans have grown and been enhanced. Some popular options are the following:

- **SEP, or simplified employee pension**—You can contribute and deduct up to 20 percent of your self-employment income. In lean years, you don't have to put anything into the account. This is the easiest self-employed plan to set up, and you can do so as late as the April filing deadline.

- **Keogh plan**—This is the self-employed equivalent of a large company retirement program. You can set up a Keogh as a profit-sharing plan or a defined benefit pension plan. A Keogh also must be in place by the end of the tax year, although you can wait until April (or later if you get a filing extension) to actually make your annual contribution. Keoghs, however, are more difficult (and costly) to administer and maintain.

- **Solo 401(k)**—This plan enables you to save much more of your self-employment earnings than do the other two plans. That also means larger deductions. Like a Keogh, a Solo-K (as they are often called) must be in place by December 31.

Your self-employment endeavor doesn't have to be your primary job.

Part- or full-time self-employment—Remember, too, that your self-employment endeavor doesn't have to be your primary job. If you are a carpenter and build furniture only on weekends, that still counts as a business, bringing with it the many tax responsibilities and breaks that a full-time entrepreneur faces.

TRUTH

30

Mortgage interest deduction

"I shall never use profanity except in discussing house rent and taxes."

—Mark Twain, author

For most of us, our home is our biggest investment. It also provides some of our biggest tax breaks.

If you have a mortgage, the pain of that monthly payment is eased each filing season when you realize just how much tax-deductible interest you've paid.

Qualified homes—Generally, home mortgage interest is any interest you pay on a loan secured by your home. This typically is your primary residence, also sometimes referred to as your main home.

The loan may be the mortgage to buy your home, a second mortgage on the property, or a line of credit or home equity loan (HELOC). In all instances, the collateral for the money you borrow is your home. If you cannot pay the debt, your lender can take your property to pay the outstanding loan.

If you're the proud owner of a second home, the interest on that loan also is deductible. But two properties is where this tax break stops.

To be eligible, or "qualified" in tax terms, your homes don't have to be strictly houses. A home also can be a condominium or cooperative apartment, a mobile home, a boat, or any similar property that has sleeping, cooking, and toilet facilities. So, if you plan to retire and travel the country in an RV, as long as it's your primary or second home, you can deduct the interest on the loan.

And in some cases, a rental property might be considered a second home. In this case, you must live in it either fourteen days out of the year or at least ten percent of the number of days you rent it for, whichever is greater. Of course, you might get more tax advantages from treating the home as a full-time rental or investment property. Check with your tax adviser to compare the tax results in each scenario.

Deduction limits—Okay. You have a qualified home (or two) and you have a loan (or loans) on the property (or properties). Now you need to take a look at how much debt you have. The amount and type of debt affects the interest deductibility.

Interest on home acquisition debt—that's tax-speak for the loan (the first mortgage) to buy your house—is deductible as long as it isn't more than $1 million ($500,000 if you're married and filing separately from your spouse). This amount applies to all acquisition debt on both your houses. So, if you got a $750,000 loan on your main house and another $300,000 mortgage to buy a vacation property, you're not going to be able to deduct all your interest.

You might have paid points to your lender to get a better loan rate. Each point represents 1 percent of your total loan, and the points usually are included in your mortgage loan amount. The total amount of points you paid is considered interest and usually is fully deductible in the tax year you purchased your home.

Points for other home-related debt, usually in the form of home equity loans or home equity lines of credit (sometimes referred to as HELOCs), also might be deductible, but unless the loan funds are used to improve the home, the points usually must be deducted over the life of the loan.

In home equity loan instances, the interest is deductible as long as your total home equity debt doesn't exceed $100,000 ($50,000 if you're married and filing separately). Your property's value also could affect the amount of interest deductible debt. The tax code says your interest write-off limit could be reduced if all your home-related debt is more than the real estate's fair market value.

So, if you're getting another loan secured by your house, crunch the numbers and again talk with your tax adviser to make sure that you can deduct as much interest payment as possible.

Timing matters, too—Tax laws changed in 1987, and the date that the new statutes went into effect regarding real estate transactions could affect your interest deduction.

If you took out a loan after Oct. 13, 1987, to buy, build, or improve your home, the $1 million and $100,000 debt limits apply. Mortgages obtained before the 1987 date are considered grandfathered debt. If you've owned your home before that date, check with your tax advisor as to how exactly the rules apply.

> In home equity loan instances, the interest is deductible as long as your total home equity debt doesn't exceed $100,000.

If you send an additional house payment before the end of the tax year, you can add that interest to the deductible amount on your upcoming return.

What if you're building your home? The IRS says you can treat a home under construction as a qualified home for up to 24 months, but only if it becomes your residence or vacation home when it's ready for occupancy.

Timing is also a tax factor in mortgage payments. If you send an additional house payment before the end of the tax year, you can add that interest to the deductible amount on your upcoming return. Although tax law generally prohibits write-offs for prepaid interest, your January payment doesn't fall into that category. Rather, mortgage payments are due at the end of the occupancy period, so the payment due January 1 covers December's principal and interest.

Paperwork required—To deduct home loan interest, you must itemize. Most homeowners do, since in addition to the mortgage interest, they also claim property taxes on Schedule A.

In some cases, however, it might not be worthwhile to itemize. This could be the case for homeowners who've owned a home for a long time and are paying more in principal than interest. So, compare your interest and other itemized deduction amounts against the standard deduction you can claim.

If you are able to deduct your mortgage interest, make sure you get a Form 1098 or your lender's substitute statement detailing, among other things, the amount of interest you paid. The IRS will get a copy, too; make sure that your Schedule A amount matches the figure tax examiners are expecting.

TRUTH

31

Writing off your property taxes

Real estate taxes are one of the most aggravating taxes around. In almost every county in almost every state, homeowners dread the arrival of their property tax bills.

Uncle Sam can't help you lower your annual home assessment, but he does provide a way that this local levy can reduce your federal tax bill. You can claim your property tax payments as itemized deductions.

No limits—Although in many deduction instances, the tax code limits how much you can claim, that's not a problem when it comes to property taxes.

Not only are all real estate taxes, regardless of whether they are collected by your state, county, city, or some other governmental taxing jurisdiction, fully deductible, but you can also deduct such taxes on all your real estate holdings.

That's right. The deduction for interest on home loans is limited to two properties, but you can write off the property taxes you pay on every property you own, not just two.

There's also no dollar limit on the amount of property taxes you can deduct. If all your property tax bills amount to $100,000, then that's how much you can claim. Of course, there is a catch. If you earn a lot of money—and with all those houses, you probably do!—your overall itemized deductions on Schedule A, of which your property taxes are part, will be reduced.

What's not a tax?—Some assessments, however, are not taxes. That means they are not deductible.

Many states and counties impose local benefit taxes for improvements to property. This includes assessments for streets, sidewalks, and sewer lines. These amounts generally aren't deductible, although charges that are for maintenance, repair, or interest charges related to those benefits are deductible.

The deduction for interest on home loans is limited to two properties, but you can write off the property taxes you pay on every property you own, not just two.

The rule of thumb is that to be deductible on your federal return, a local tax must be charged uniformly against all property in the jurisdiction and be based on the assessed value of the real estate.

Some property tax statements delineate these different types of charges, but most do not. Congress has discussed requiring more detailed reporting by property taxing entities, but until that happens, check with your tax assessor-collector, and your tax advisor, if you have questions about a charge and whether it might be deductible. The IRS says that if you cannot determine what part of the tax is deductible, then you cannot claim any of the amount on your federal return.

There also are some assessments that clearly are not deductible as real estate taxes. They include the following:

- Trash and garbage pickup fees

- Transfer taxes, or stamp taxes, usually found on your home purchase closing statement

- Rent increases due to your landlord's higher real estate taxes

- Homeowner association charges

A deduction if you itemize … or not—In most cases, you must itemize to deduct your home's property taxes. The amount is entered in the "Taxes You Paid" section of Schedule A.

However, a law enacted in 2008 now allows some homeowners to include at least a part of their property tax payments in their standard deduction. Single filers can add up to $500 in property taxes to their standard deduction amount; married couples filing a joint return can include up to $1,000. Note the "up to" phrase—if your property tax bill is less than $500 or $1,000, you can claim only as must as your actual, smaller tax bill.

Note, however, that this new law applies only to 2008 and 2009 tax returns. Keep an eye on Congress, since once a tax break is on the books, federal lawmakers have a tendency to extend them.

Taxes when you buy—When you bought your home, you probably paid some property taxes.

The home buyer and seller must divide the real estate taxes according to the number of days that each owned the property. The seller pays the taxes up to the sale date; the buyer pays them starting that day and through the end of the tax year. These deductible amounts are detailed on your closing statement.

Escrow versus actually paid—Your house payment likely is a combination of several things: the loan principal and interest, insurance coverage, and property taxes. The amounts attributable to insurance and property taxes go into an escrow account from which your lender pays the bills when they are due.

Although you are paying into your property tax escrow account throughout the year, you can only deduct the actual amount of taxes that are paid to your taxing authority in that tax year.

The Form 1098 or substitute statement that your lender sends you early each year will detail, among other things, the amount of taxes paid on your behalf during the tax year.

Limits on overall deductions—Although there is no limit on the amount of property taxes you can claim or the number of homes on which they are assessed, you may face a limit on your overall itemized deductions.

> Although there is no limit on the amount of property taxes you can claim or the number of homes on which they are assessed, you may face a limit on your overall itemized deductions.

This applies when your adjusted gross income is greater than a certain amount, adjusted annually for inflation and noted at the bottom of Schedule A. In this case, the value of all your itemized deductions, including your property tax write-off, will be reduced by 1 percent of the amount that your AGI exceeds the threshold. The good news: In 2010, the phase-out itself is phased out, and you get back full value of all your deductions regardless of the amount.

32

Increasing your home's tax basis

When you sell your home, you naturally want to get top dollar. But from a tax standpoint, that could be costly.

True, most homeowners find that when they sell, they won't owe any tax on the profit. As long as the money they make on the transaction comes in at or below the exclusion amounts of $250,000 for single taxpayers, and twice that for couples who file jointly, the IRS doesn't get a cent. (You can read more on the home-sale tax break in Truth 33, "Home-sale tax exclusion.")

But if you're worried that you might exceed the sale-exclusion limits, your home itself might offer a solution. Some structural changes or improvements you've made to the place could change your sale's tax situation for the better.

Determining your home's basis—Before you can determine your precise profit and any possible tax consequences, you need to know your "basis" in your home.

Basis is your investment in a property, be it real estate or an investment such as stock. This usually is the amount you paid for it. You then must calculate your adjusted basis, which is any increase or decrease in the property's value. Finally, you subtract your adjusted basis from your sale proceeds to arrive at your net profit. The profit is the amount in which the IRS is interested.

Your home's basis is determined by how you acquired it. If you bought or built it, your basis is primarily its cost. This includes the purchase price and certain settlement or closing costs. If you built your home, your purchase price can include construction costs. If the house is left to you upon someone's death, its basis is the real estate's fair market value when you inherited it.

If, however, while you owned your home, you made some improvements to the property, they might be able to increase your adjusted basis enough to ensure that you don't encounter any tax issues upon sale.

> Some structural changes or improvements you've made to the place could change your sale's tax situation for the better.

Tax-valuable home improvements—You can add to your home's basis the cost of improvements made to the property as long as they do one of three things, as follows:

1. Add to the value of your home.
2. Prolong its useful life.
3. Adapt it to new uses.

The changes are limited to a degree by the tax code, but mostly any way you can imagine to improve your property will count when it comes to calculating adjusted basis.

You can turn your unfinished basement into a recreation room, install new wiring throughout your house for a complete residential sound system, or add a new garage for your third car.

You don't have to stay within your home's walls. Improvements to the property around your house count, too. Putting up a new fence, adding a deck, or paving your gravel driveway are basis-building home improvements.

Here are some basis-adjusting improvements that are specifically listed by the IRS:

- **Additions**—Bedroom, bathroom, deck, garage, porch, and patio.

- **Interior upgrades**—Built-in appliances, kitchen modernization, flooring, and wall-to-wall carpeting.

- **Heating and air conditioning**—Heating system, furnace, central air conditioning, duct work, central humidifier, and filtration system.

- **Plumbing**—Septic system, water heater, soft water system, and filtration system.

- **Insulation**—Attic, walls, floors, pipes, and duct work.

- **Lawn and grounds**—Landscaping, driveway, walkway, fence, retaining wall, sprinkler system, and swimming pool.

- **Miscellaneous**—Storm windows, doors, new roof, central vacuum, wiring upgrades, satellite dish, and security system.

Repairs versus improvements—As a homeowner, you know that repairs take up much of your time and money. Although they are necessary, the IRS does not consider routine maintenance as adding value to your home or prolonging its life. Therefore, you cannot add these costs to the basis of your property.

This often is a confusing distinction. For example, although your new roof might have had its origins in a repair job, the IRS agrees that the new, complete shingling job prolongs the life of your home. That makes it a home improvement.

However, projects such as interior or exterior repainting, fixing gutters, repairing leaks or plastering, or replacing broken window panes are repairs in the eyes of the IRS. These tasks simply keep your home in an ordinary, efficient operating condition.

There is one way the IRS enables you to include repair costs as items that you can add to your home's basis. If projects that normally would be considered repairs are done as part of an extensive remodeling or restoration of your home, then they become improvements. For example, if your home is damaged due to a casualty loss, such as a hurricane, you can increase your basis by the amount you spend on repairs that restore the property to its pre-storm condition.

Your local government's actions also could add to your home's basis. Many states and counties collect local benefit taxes for improvements to property, such as assessments for streets, sidewalks, and sewer lines. Although these taxes cannot be deducted as can other property taxes (more details on this tax break can be found in Truth 31, "Writing off your property taxes"), you can increase the cost basis of your property by the amount of the assessment.

Proving your improvements—As with every action that reduces your tax liability, when it comes to items that affect your home's basis, keep good records. You'll need all those amounts to compute your adjusted basis and net profit when you sell. After the property transfer, the general tax record-keeping rule is to hang onto your tax-filing documentation, including home-improvement receipts, for three years after your return's due date.

TRUTH

33

Home-sale tax exclusion

On May 7, 1997, tax life for home sellers changed dramatically and for the better.

Before that day, to avoid tax on home-sale profits you had to use the sale money to buy another property. If you happened to be 55 or older back then, you were able to keep up to $125,000 in profits tax-free. But that was a one-time exclusion, and you had to fill out the proper paperwork to prove that you didn't have to pay Uncle Sam some of your money.

But since that May day, home sellers have been able to keep up to $250,000 of home-sale profit, or $500,000 for married couples filing a joint return, out of IRS hands.

Now you don't have to be a certain age. There are no forms to fill out. You simply have to meet some simple residency requirements.

Owning, living in the house—This generous tax exclusion is available as long as you both owned and used the home as your principal residence for two of the five years before the sale.

The ownership factor is clear. Either you've paid for the home in full or are paying a mortgage on the place. If you are legally responsible for the home debt, for tax purposes you are the owner.

The primary residence rule also is obvious. This is the house in which you and your family live most of the time. It's the address that's on your voter's registration, driver's license, and car titles. Utilities are hooked up, and the electric and gas company bills come to that mailbox. That home's address is the one that's on your tax return.

You'll probably meet the requirement that you live in the home at least two years of the five years before you sell by staying there two consecutive years. However, that's not a requirement. The ownership and use periods don't have to be concurrent. The two years may consist of 24 full months or 730 days, and short absences, such as for a summer vacation, count as periods of use. So, you can live in your home for six months, move to Italy for a year, come back home, and then stay there another year and a half and meet the sale-exclusion requirement.

You also can include in your "home sale exclusion amount" any gain from the sale of vacant land that was used as part of the residence. In this case, the land sale must occur within two years before or after the sale of the principal residence.

You can claim the exclusion on as many homes as you own as long as you meet the residency requirement. However, you can only claim the tax break for subsequent qualifying home sales once every two years.

Exceptions and partial exclusion— Sometimes, you have to sell your home before you've lived there for the tax-required two years. In these cases, you might be eligible for a partial exclusion.

The IRS says when you are forced to sell a home because of special conditions or unforeseen circumstances, you're eligible for a prorated tax-free profit.

The IRS says when you are forced to sell a home because of special conditions or unforeseen circumstances, you're eligible for a prorated tax-free profit.

You must first calculate the amount of time that you met the two-year use test. For example, you're in your house for only a year when your company transfers you to another city. That means you've lived there for 12 of the 24 required residency months, or fractionally, 12/24 (or one-half) of the tax exclusion time. You netted the full $250,000 exclusion amount when you sold the property, but you can exclude only half, or $125,000, of that gain from your income.

So, what counts as an unforeseen circumstance? The IRS includes such events as the following:

- Death

- Divorce or legal separation

- Job loss that entitles the homeowner to collect unemployment

- Employment changes that make it difficult for the homeowner to meet mortgage and basic living expenses

- Multiple births from the same pregnancy

If any of these situations occur to you, your spouse, a property co-owner, or a family member who lives in the home, you qualify for the partial exclusion if you must sell your house.

Military personnel get an even better exception to the two-year residency rule since redeployments often make it difficult for servicemen and women to meet that requirement.

You also can claim a partial exclusion if you had to sell because of damage to your home due to a natural or man-made disaster or your property was taken by a local government under eminent domain law.

Military personnel get an even better exception to the two-year residency rule since redeployments often make it difficult for servicemen and women to meet that requirement. In these cases, military personnel are exempted from the two-year use requirement for up to 10 years. They qualify for the full exclusion whenever they must move due to armed forces service commitments.

Second home sale complications—However, a new law that arrives when the calendar flips to 2009 closes a once-popular home-sale exclusion loophole.

Previously, owners of multiple homes could sell a main residence, claim the full tax exclusion, move into a second property, live in it as the principal residence for two years, and then sell and reap the full home sale-exclusion amount.

A provision in the Housing Assistance Act of 2008 puts a stop to part of that process. You still can convert a second home to your main residence. And you still can live in the place long enough to get a tax break when you sell. But, in most instances, you won't get the full $250,000 or $500,000 exclusion amount. Now you will owe tax on part of the sale money that is attributable to the time, after January 1, 2009, that the home was used as second property—for example, as a vacation home or rental property.

As the effects of this new law begin to be felt, look for the IRS to issue regulations and instructions on how to deal with second-to-primary home conversions and sales.

TRUTH

34

Capital gains rules and rates

You stuck to your investment plan, and it's paid off. You now have a nice nest egg.

Now you need to make sure you don't sabotage your portfolio by making moves that could produce costly tax consequences.

When you sell a capital asset, such as a stock, piece of real estate, or any other investment holding, the difference between your asset's basis (its initial cost plus other expenses incurred while you owned it) and the amount you sell it for, will give you a capital gain or a capital loss.

Although a loss can sometimes be useful (more on this circumstance in Truth 35, "How bad investments can pay off"), the goal is to come away with a gain. And timing your sale, when possible, can determine whether your gain will be taxed at the lowest possible rate.

The many capital gains rates—When you hear the term "capital gains," you probably think of the preferable tax rate that most investors get when they sell an asset for a profit.

That's true. But actually, there are four capital gains rates, ranging from 0 percent to 28 percent. In most cases, one of the capital gains rates will give you a smaller tax bill, as long as you follow the tax code rules.

Capital gains (and losses) can be short-term or long-term. They get their designations based on how long you've owned the asset. When you own an asset for more than a year (366 days or longer), any gain you earn, or loss you suffer, on its sale is long-term. Assets held for a year or less are short-term.

Long-term transactions are the investor's tax goal; they will take a smaller tax bite out of your earnings. When you make a profit on a short-term sale, you'll owe taxes at your ordinary income tax rate, which could be as high as 35 percent. The top long-term capital gain rate is 28 percent, but for typical asset sales, the tax rate is just 15 percent.

There are four capital gains rates, ranging from 0 percent to 28 percent.

If waiting to sell an asset fits into your overall investment strategy, then holding the stock or property long enough for it to qualify as a long-term investment could make a real difference in your tax bill.

Your capital gains rate also depends on your income. Investors whose overall adjusted gross income is in the lower ordinary tax brackets will get the best capital gains rates. Some taxpayers, in fact, will owe no capital gains taxes at all.

Finally, the type of investment you sell also could affect your capital gains rate.

0 percent rate—Yes, it's true. If your income falls into the 10 percent and 15 percent ordinary tax brackets, then you might be able to sell long-term assets without any tax liability.

The 0 percent rate for capital gains took effect with the 2008 tax year, replacing the previous 5 percent rate. This no-tax rate continues through 2010.

There are, however, a few instances when the 0 percent rate is not allowed. To discourage higher-income investors from shifting assets to young people who usually are in the lower tax brackets, the "kiddie tax" law (details in Truth 38, "Accounting for the kiddie tax") specifically prohibits young investors from getting the zero percent rate.

On the other end of the age spectrum, older individuals may be eligible for the 0 percent rate based on their smaller retirement incomes. But be careful if you rely primarily on Social Security; income from untaxed capital gains could affect the taxation of that government benefit.

15 percent rate—The 15 percent rate is the one that most investors pay on long-term profits. It applies to gains received by individuals who are in the 25 percent or higher tax brackets. This rate previously was 20 percent. The rate cut, however, is temporary. Unless Congress extends it, this rate will go to 20 percent in 2011.

25 percent rate—The 25 percent rate applies to part of the gain from selling certain real estate investments that were depreciated. You might see these referred to as Section 1250 gains. This higher tax rate allows the government to recapture some of the tax breaks you got over the years through the accelerated depreciation. In dealing with investment real estate, it's usually a good idea to consult a tax professional to make sure you don't overlook any tax breaks or liabilities.

28 percent rate—The 28 percent rate applies to two types of long-term capital gain property: certain small business stock and collectibles.

The eligible small business stock that falls into this capital gains category has a longer holding period of five years and qualified for a special 50 percent exclusion that enabled you to keep half of your gain out of income. The rest of your gain is taxed at the 28 percent rate. This also is an area of the tax code where getting professional counsel is a wise move.

Rather than paper or, more common nowadays, electronic securities, some investors prefer that their assets take a more tangible form. They put their money into art, antiques, gems, stamps, coins, baseball cards, or select wines. But that choice means they pay a higher tax price. When these collectible assets are sold for a gain, they are subject to the 28 percent capital gains rate.

Keep an eye on Congress—Although the current lower capital gains rates of 0 and 15 percent are scheduled to continue through 2010, remember that what Congress gave, Congress can take away.

In January 2009, a new president will be sworn in, along with new members of Congress. Changes on Capitol Hill could produce revisions to the capital gains and other tax laws before they expire at the end of 2010.

Although tax considerations should be a part of your investment strategy, they shouldn't be the only or predominant factor.

Also remember that although tax considerations should be a part of your investment strategy, they shouldn't be the only or predominant factor. Talk with your financial and tax advisors about which money moves, such as selling some holdings or rebalancing your portfolio, best fit your overall investment plan, and then deal with any tax consequences.

35

How bad investments can pay off

No one wants to lose money on an investment. But when it comes to taxes, a loss could turn out to be a good thing.

If you've made money via capital gains, a loss on another asset sale could help reduce or possibly eliminate your tax liability.

If you have no capital gains to offset, a portion of your losses can be applied against your ordinary income.

And if you have substantial losses, they could pay off on tax returns for several years.

Determining your basis—The first step in making use of a stock sale loss is determining the asset's "basis." Your initial basis is what you originally paid for the asset. It's then adjusted by accounting for other expenses incurred while you owned it.

Basis is crucial for tax purposes. It will directly affect the amount of gain or loss that you incur when you sell an asset. When you sell any capital asset, its gain or loss come from the difference between its selling price and its adjusted basis.

You start with the price you paid for the security, and then account for activity such as reinvested dividends and capital gain distributions and stock splits. You even can, in most cases, take into account fees you paid to acquire or redeem fund shares.

The final figure is the adjusted basis, which will determine how much of a gain or loss you'll realize when you sell.

> When you sell any capital asset, its gain or loss come from the difference between its selling price and its adjusted basis.

"Harvesting" your losses—Most of us have no problem selling a stock that gives us a capital gain. However, it's often more difficult to let go of one that has lost value.

Maybe you have an emotional attachment to the security; it's the stock of a company where you, or your family, worked for many years. Perhaps you took a flyer on the stock and now don't want to admit that you should have done better market homework.

But selling the asset and recording the loss can put a poor investment to better tax use.

Timing your sale—A key consideration is when to sell. Although this choice should be made primarily with regard to your

> Selling the asset and recording the loss can put a poor investment to better tax use.

overall investment strategy, the timing of your loss will determine exactly how tax valuable it is to you.

Just as capital gains are either short- or long-term, so are losses. If you sell a losing stock you've owned for a year or less, that constitutes a short-term loss. Stocks that you've owned for more than a year and then are sold at a loss are long-term losses.

The distinction is important because your capital gains and losses aren't simply dumped into one investment bucket. You use your short-term losses to first offset short-term gains; the same process is used for long-term investments.

When you use your capital loss amounts to reduce the corresponding capital gains, any leftover capital losses can next be subtracted from the other type of capital gain. For example, you have $3,000 in short-term losses, but only $1,000 worth of short-term gains. You can apply the extra $2,000 short-term loss to any long-term gain you have.

If you have any capital losses left over after using them against gains, up to $3,000 of that excess loss amount can be deducted against your ordinary income, your salary, and other earnings. If you have more than $3,000 in excess losses, you can carry that amount forward to apply it to gains or ordinary income in future tax years. Just make sure you hang onto your tax and investment records.

You also can use your capital losses against ordinary income in tax years when you have no capital gains to offset. In these cases, the $3,000 per year limit still applies. But you can take as many years as necessary to use up the excess loss amounts.

0 percent considerations—If you're eligible for the 0 percent rate on capital gains, you might want to examine your loss-taking strategy.

Through 2010, taxpayers in the 10 percent and 15 percent tax brackets don't owe any taxes on long-term capital gains. So, selling losing long-term stocks during this time means that you don't get the maximum benefit of your losses.

Talk with your tax and investment advisors as to how some investment moves might be maximized from a tax standpoint.

True, you still can use up to $3,000 of the losses to reduce your ordinary income amount, but it might be worth postponing the taking of those losses until a future tax year when they could be used to more fully offset any taxable capital gains.

Of course, the tax treatment of your asset sales is just one factor to consider. If your investment strategy calls for you to sell a particular stock, regardless of its relative tax value, then you should do so. But you also should talk with your tax and investment advisors as to how some investment moves might be maximized from a tax standpoint.

Losses that aren't deductible—Finally, keep in mind that not all asset sale losses provide tax advantages. Losses incurred upon the sale of personal-use property, such as your home or car, are not deductible.

TRUTH

36

Reporting investment
income

There are two bad things about making money off of your investments: paying taxes and filling out the paperwork to pay the taxes.

Your filing duties depend upon how much you make and the type of earnings you receive. And, in addition to another form or two to send to the IRS, you'll likely have some worksheets to mess with, too.

But just keep reminding yourself that the added calculations will help lower your tax bill.

Interest and dividends—If your earnings consist only of interest and dividend payments and the amount of each is $1,500 or less, you can report that income directly on your Form 1040 or 1040A.

If these earnings are more, then you'll have to fill out Schedule A if you're a Form 1040 filer or Schedule 1 if your return is Form 1040A.

Note that the $1,500 threshold is for each category. If you have $1,499 in interest and $1,499 in dividends, then you don't need the schedules.

You also must be specific in reporting the types of dividends you receive. Ordinary dividends are taxed at your regular income tax rate. Qualified dividends, however, receive special treatment and are taxed at the lower capital gains rate. The tax classification of "qualified dividends" was created in 2003 and applies to dividends that you own for a specific time during the tax year.

You'll notice on your year-end account statements that your investment manager has calculated, and listed separately, the portion of your overall earnings that meet the qualified dividend requirements. The differentiation also will be shown on your Form 1099-DIV or the substitute annual tax statement your investment manager sends you.

Distributions only—If your only investment earnings for the tax year were from capital gains distributions, you'll again report the amount directly on your 1040 or 1040A. These are payments that are made to shareholders of mutual funds or other regulated investment companies as part of the proceeds from fund activity throughout the year.

With an individual stock, you decide when to buy or sell. But with a mutual fund, the fund manager has control over selling assets. When the transaction produces a gain for the fund, each shareholder's portion is passed along as capital gains distributions. The largest capital gains distribution usually is paid at the end of the tax year.

The tax upside of these payments is that they are treated as long-term capital gains, meaning they receive the most favorable tax rate.

The tax downside is that you could receive taxable capital gain distributions even if the fund itself lost value during the tax year.

Capital gains—When you sell an asset, either a security or investment real estate, you'll become well acquainted with Schedule D, Capital Gains and Losses. As the form's name indicates, you'll need to complete it when you make or lose money on an investment property transaction.

This multicolumned two-page document can be intimidating, especially if you're tackling the paper version instead of using computer software. But the details it seeks can help you reduce your tax bill.

If you have a gain on a long-term asset—that is, one you held for more than a year—then that profit generally is taxed at a lower rate. For taxpayers in the four upper-income tax brackets (25, 28, 33, and 35 percent), the long-term capital gains rate typically is 15 percent; filers in the 10 and 15 percent brackets will owe no tax on their long-term gains.

Reporting a loss also could offer tax savings. You can use a capital loss to offset corresponding capital gains or even some of your ordinary income.

Schedule D collects your transaction data—the asset or assets sold, acquisition date, selling date, sales price, asset cost, or basis—and then you report your gain or loss. This is done separately on the form for both short-term and long-term assets.

When you sell an asset, either a security or investment real estate, you'll become well-acquainted with Schedule D, Capital Gains and Losses.

Don't overlook mutual fund transactions. When you liquidate a fund, it obviously is a sale of a capital asset with tax consequences to be reported to the IRS. So is exchanging one fund for another within the same company. Such reallocations are, in the IRS view, sales.

Other capital gains—In addition to reporting your typical investment gains or losses, you use Schedule D to let the IRS know of transactions that are subject to the other (25 percent and 28 percent) capital gains rates. These include gains from the sale of collectibles or certain small business stock, as well as transactions involving business property that was depreciated.

If the sale of your home netted you more than the exclusion amounts of $250,000 for single taxpayers or $500,000 for married couples filing jointly, that gain also would be reported on Schedule D.

Record keeping—Although you'll transfer the information from your 1099 forms and other investment statements to Schedule D, be sure to hang onto those forms.

Accurate records that show the basis and adjusted basis of your property are critical if you need to answer any questions the IRS might have about your gains or losses.

For ease of record keeping, check with your investment companies. Many allow you to download the documents. Many financial and tax software programs also let you import data about trades and transactions.

If you are carrying forward excess capital losses to future tax years, hang onto your returns to keep track of this amount.

TRUTH

37

Wash sale rules

Sometimes stock transactions make you want to wash your hands of all investing. Other times, you're more philosophic and view gains and losses that "wash each other out" as just part of the process.

But if you try to time a stock sale and repurchase to take a tax loss but hang onto the asset or one similar to it, the IRS will crack down on you for violating its "wash sale rule."

The rule was created to keep investors from gaming the tax and investment systems. Here's what the IRS wants to prevent:

You own a stock that you believe will, in the long term, be a good investment. However, at the moment, it has dropped in value so that if you sell it, you can use it as a capital loss against gains or ordinary income. But to keep the asset within your portfolio, you buy it back shortly after your tax-motivated sale.

Not so fast, says the IRS. A wash sale occurs when you sell or trade stock or securities at a loss, and within 30 days, either before or after the sale, you do the following:

■ Buy substantially identical stock or securities

■ Acquire substantially identical stock or securities in a fully taxable trade

■ Acquire a contract or option to buy substantially identical stock or securities

Note the 30-days-before provision. You can't get around wash sale prohibitions by first buying new shares of the stock and then selling your older shares at a loss. That means the complete wash sale restriction period is 61 calendar days: 30 days before the sale, the day of the sale, and 30 days after the sale.

And even if you don't actually take ownership of the new stock within the restricted 61 days, wash sale rules still apply to contracts or options to acquire the same or similar stock.

Wash consequences—If you violate the wash sale rule, the immediate consequence is that you lose the loss claim on your tax return. This could be costly if you had sold some assets that produced a gain.

148

Normally, when you have income from an investment, you can minimize the amount upon which you owe taxes by subtracting the amount of losses you suffered on other asset sales. But if your losses are from stock that you repurchased too quickly, in this wash-sale situation, you're not allowed to use those loss amounts to reduce your taxable gains.

If you violate the wash sale rule, the immediate consequence is that you lose the loss claim on your tax return.

The amount of your disallowed loss is not lost, just postponed. The loss amount is added to the basis of the replacement stock you purchased, so you get the benefit of the loss when you sell the new shares.

For example, you buy 100 shares of X stock for $1,000. You sell the shares for $750, and within 30 days of the sale, you buy 100 new shares of X stock for $800. Because you bought substantially identical stock, you cannot deduct your loss of $250. However, you add the disallowed $250 loss to the cost of the $800 cost of the new share stock, giving you a new basis of $1,050.

When you sell that second batch of X shares for $1,500, your taxable capital gain is $450. If you did not have the added $250, your gain would have been $700 ($1,500 minus $800). So, the loss that you weren't able to claim earlier now helps lower your subsequent taxable gain.

Finally, the holding period of the stock you sold is now added to the ownership time of your just-purchased replacement stock. This provision, in most cases, will ensure that you aren't able to convert a long-term loss into a short-term one. Usually, short-term losses are more valuable, since they help reduce or eliminate short-term gain that is taxed at regular income tax rates, which could be as high as 35 percent.

Defining identical—The wash sale rule prohibits repurchase of "substantially identical" stock or securities. Obviously, this means if you sold Home Depot shares, you cannot buy replacement Home Depot shares. But will shares in competing Lowe's be too close for comfort in the IRS's eyes? Possibly.

Ordinarily, stocks or securities of one corporation are not considered substantially identical to stocks or securities of another corporation.

The IRS says you must consider all the facts and circumstances in your particular case. Ordinarily, stocks or securities of one corporation are not considered substantially identical to stocks or securities of another corporation. Under this analysis, the Lowe's shares should be acceptable.

The distinction gets a bit trickier with mutual funds. For example, you sold all your shares in an environmental services fund to claim the loss. But you believe that the environmental sector holds great return potential, so you pick up shares in an ecologically oriented fund offered by another fund family. Are the funds similar enough to set off IRS wash sale alarms?

Possibly. However, there are no hard and fast rules with regard to mutual fund similarities and the wash sale rule. Fund managers take different approaches to the investments, so you might be able to argue that the two funds are not similar enough to violate the rules. If you want to make such a purchase, be aware that it could be questioned, and disallowed.

Finally, don't worry about sales and repurchases of similar or even identical stock when the transaction produces a gain. The wash sale provisions apply only to sales that result in a capital loss.

TRUTH

38

Accounting for the kiddie tax

You've probably heard of the "kiddie tax." Perhaps you're aware that it has something to do with a youngster's investment income.

Maybe you think it's a special tax benefit for these forward-thinking youngsters who are already building a nice portfolio.

You would be wrong. Despite the nickname, the so-called kiddie tax doesn't treat young investors' with kid gloves. The tax is, in fact, designed to make sure the IRS gets as much tax money from such investments as possible.

The kiddie tax was created in 1986 because some parents had been putting investment accounts in a child's name so that the earnings would be taxed at the youth's low tax bracket rather than at the adults' higher rate.

To stop the income shifting, the law was changed and dubbed the kiddie tax. It now requires that at least some of a dependent child's investment money be taxed at the parents' higher rate.

The key kiddie tax rules—There are a few basic things to keep in mind when it comes to the kiddie tax.

First, it applies, in most cases, to youngsters younger than 19. Older kids could get caught in the kiddie tax net if they're attending college.

For the kiddie tax to apply, the youngster must be a dependent. Children who provide more than half of their own support are not subject to its rules.

The kiddie tax only affects unearned income. When a child has enough earned income, either from wages or self-employment, to require that he or she file a return, those earnings are still taxed at the youth's tax rate.

There is a threshold, usually adjusted annually to reflect inflation, under which the kiddie tax doesn't apply.

> The kiddie tax was created in 1986 because some parents had been putting investment accounts in a child's name so that the earnings would be taxed at the youth's low tax bracket rather than at the adults' higher rate.

Added earnings mean added taxes—Tax law still provides favorable treatment for some of a child's investment earnings. A small amount—for 2008 tax purposes, it was $900; the IRS decides each fall whether the figure needs to be adjusted to account for inflation—is tax-free.

Then the next equal amount of unearned income is taxed at the child's tax bracket rate. In 2008, for example, a child could make up to $1,800 from stocks, bonds, CDs, and savings accounts and still not owe Uncle Sam very much.

> In 2008, for example, a child could make up to $1,800 from stocks, bonds, CDs, and savings accounts and still not owe Uncle Sam very much.

But once the earnings go over that combined nontaxed/child's tax rate amount, the IRS will collect on that money using the parents' tax rate.

Age is important—When the kiddie tax was first put into the tax code, it was in effect until the young investor turned 14. After that birthday, taxation went back to the child's rate.

It's unclear why lawmakers originally chose age 14. Perhaps Congressional number crunchers figured by that age, a child was likely to have an after-school or weekend job through which he or she made enough money, earned and unearned, to guarantee that the Treasury would get a decent tax cut anyway.

But in recent years, as Congress and the Administration have struggled to come up with as much revenue as possible to help fill a growing deficit gap, the kiddie tax age has increased. In 2005, a tax law change bumped it up to age 18. The increases didn't stop there.

Now the kiddie tax provisions taxing a youngster's investment income at his or her parents' rate stay in effect until the youth turns 19 or 24 if the youngster is a full-time student.

Paying the kiddie tax—When a youth's unearned income triggers the kiddie tax, the child and parents have some filing decisions to make.

The youngster can file a return. As for the investment income that triggered the need to file, he or she will have to also complete Form 8615 and attach it to the Form 1040 or Form 1040A.

Although it is the child's return, you'll see that the form asks for the name and Social Security number of the parent who is listed first on the adult return. This is so IRS examiners can double-check the parents' filing to make sure that the tax applied on the child's return is figured at the correct rate.

If, however, you and your child want to avoid sending in a return for the youngster, you might be able to include your youngster's investment income on your return. You do so by filing Form 8814, Parents' Election to Report Child's Interest and Dividends, along with your Form 1040.

This option, however, has an earnings limit; if your child's earnings from interest, dividends, and capital gain distributions hits or exceeds that limit, the child must file his or her own return. You'll find the earnings limit on Form 8814.

If you have two or more children who are subject to the kiddie tax, each child's tax situation must be dealt with individually, either with their own return and Form 8615 or a separate Form 8814 for each child submitted with the parents' return.

If you have two or more children who are subject to the kiddie tax, each child's tax situation must be dealt with individually, either with their own return and Form 8615 or a separate Form 8814 for each child submitted with the parents' return.

Look out for unintended consequences—Parents and children should run the numbers on both Form 8615 and Form 8814 to see which filing method will give your family a better combined tax result.

You also need to keep in mind that adding a child's investment earnings to your tax return could increase your adjusted gross income to a point where it could cost you some tax benefits. For example, the child's income could cause you to have too much money to qualify for some deductions or credits. Even if you still qualify for the breaks, the addition to your income could cause them to be reduced.

TRUTH

39

Individual retirement accounts

"Philosophy teaches a man that he can't take it with him; taxes teach him he can't leave it behind either."

—Mignon McLaughlin, author

Individual retirement accounts were created in 1974 as a way to help individuals without workplace pensions save for retirement. The basic format of the original, traditional IRA has remained the same. You contribute a certain amount each year, and your account grows tax-deferred until you take out the money upon retirement.

But over the years, as workplaces and employee needs changed, so have IRAs. New versions have appeared, and extra contributions options have been added. Which IRA works best for you will depend upon your personal financial and tax situation, so look carefully at all your options.

Traditional IRA—Traditional IRAs are the granddaddy of personal retirement plans. They were created for workers who did not have an on-the-job retirement plan. Soon, however, lawmakers saw the benefit of opening up this savings option.

Anyone younger than age 70½ who earns money can put a portion of that income, as late as the April tax return filing deadline, into a traditional IRA. The maximum contribution level has grown from $1,500 in 1974 to $5,000 in 2008. Another recent development is the catch-up provision, which allows workers age 50 or older to contribute more. In 2008, older earners could put up to $6,000 into an IRA. Both regular and catch-up contribution limits are bumped up annually if the level of inflation warrants an increase.

Keep in mind that the earnings limits are the maximum possible amount you can put into your IRA. Your actual contributions also are restricted by exactly how much money you earn. You must, in most cases, receive wages or a salary to be eligible for an IRA, and you cannot contribute more than you earn.

Age also is a factor with traditional IRAs. Once you turn 70½, you no longer can contribute to an account, even if you still are earning income. In fact, once you reach that milestone, you must start taking some money out of your IRA.

> Anyone younger than age 70½ who earns money can put a portion of that income, as late as the April tax return filing deadline, into a traditional IRA.

Traditional IRAs are tax-deferred, not tax-free, accounts. When you eventually receive distributions, you will owe taxes on any deductible contributions you made, as well as on the account's earnings. Those taxes will be assessed at your ordinary income tax rate, which could be as high as 35 percent.

Deductible versus nondeductible IRAs—One of the major attractions of a traditional IRA is the possibility that you can deduct your contributions.

However, that option is no longer available to everyone. A contribution's deductibility depends on whether you, or your spouse, have a qualified retirement plan at work and how much money you make. Earn over a certain amount (check www.IRS.gov for the annual limitations), and your deduction will be reduced or possibly eliminated.

Roth IRA rules—In 1998, another individual retirement account was born: the Roth IRA. With this account, you don't have to worry about your income limiting your IRA deduction; no Roth IRA contributions are deductible.

The loss of a deduction is offset by the fact that when you take money out of a Roth IRA, if you've had the account for at least five years, you won't owe any taxes on those withdrawals.

In addition to tax-free distributions, a Roth IRA offers other benefits. You can contribute to the account regardless of your age. And you can leave the money in a Roth as long as you want. Roth funds aren't subject to the required age 70½ distribution rule, meaning your entire account can keep earning longer.

As with a traditional IRA, you must have earned income to open a Roth. And the regular and catch-up contribution amounts are the same as for a traditional account.

Roth accounts, however, do have some limits, specifically when it comes to your income. Although you must earn money to contribute to any IRA, if you make a lot, you won't be able to open or contribute to a Roth account. Again, check the IRS web page for the tax year's specific earnings limits.

Converting to a Roth IRA—If you're eligible, you can open a new Roth or, if you have an existing traditional IRA, you can roll over that money to a Roth IRA.

The advantage of rolling a traditional IRA to a Roth account is that the transferred money then gains tax-free status.

The advantage of rolling a traditional IRA to a Roth account is that the transferred money then gains tax-free status. But there are a few considerations to get to this more favorable tax status.

You can only convert a traditional IRA to a Roth if you make $100,000 or less, regardless of your filing status. More importantly, you must pay applicable taxes on the traditional IRA money that you convert. Depending upon how much you have in your traditional IRA, that could be costly.

You can ease that tax bite somewhat by converting your traditional IRA money incrementally over several years. Or if you can wait until 2010, you can completely convert your traditional IRA to a Roth and spread conversion taxes over two tax years, when you file returns in 2011 and 2012. Even better, the income conversion limit is waived for folks who convert accounts in 2010.

Before turning your traditional IRA into a Roth, make sure the change is worth it. The conversion should ultimately give you more money, not just tax-free cash. And you want to have money from other sources with which you can pay any conversion taxes. If you take the money out of your IRA to pay the IRS, you're reducing your overall nest egg.

IRA record keeping—Documentation is especially important if you have a traditional IRA containing both deductible and nondeductible contributions. You'll eventually owe tax on those deductible amounts, so you must be able to determine just how much money falls into that category to guard against overpaying the IRS.

IRS Form 8606 can help here. Use it to report your already taxed, nondeductible contributions. It'll help you figure your tax bill when you start taking money out of your traditional IRA.

TRUTH

40

Company retirement plans

Company retirement plans used to be primarily defined benefit plans. That meant that your employer set up the program and paid most of the costs. You got certain, or defined, amounts upon retiring from the company.

Now, however, most businesses offer "defined contribution plans." As the name suggests, your eventual retirement amount relies more heavily on your personal contributions to the plan.

Your employer might match at least some of your contributions, but the other major component is the tax code, which enables you to defer taxes on your company retirement funds and reduce your income tax a bit in the process.

401(k) plans—The most common type of defined contribution plan is a 401(k), named for the section of the tax code that created and governs it. If you work for an educational institution or a nonprofit, you might have a 403(b) plan, those workplaces' version of the private-sector 401(k).

You decide what percentage of your pay to contribute to the account. That money is deducted from your paychecks and deposited directly to your 401(k). Because the money comes out of your pay before federal and state income taxes are calculated, you get some immediate tax savings simply from participating in the plan.

In addition to the current income tax advantages, your 401(k) contributions grow tax-free until withdrawal. Thanks to the compounding effect of regular paycheck contributions, you could end up with a sizable nest egg.

Keep in mind, though, that you'll eventually owe tax, at your ordinary income tax rate, when you start taking money out of your 401(k).

How much to contribute—There are limits, set both by the federal government and your employer, on how much you can contribute to a 401(k).

The government amounts are usually large enough that most workers don't have to worry about bumping into them. For example, in 2008 you could defer up to $15,500 in a 401(k). If you were age 50 or older, you were allowed to contribute an extra $5,000 catch-up amount. These amounts are adjusted annually for inflation; check www.IRS.gov for the latest amounts.

160

Your company also can set contribution limits, so the total amount you might be able to put into your 401(k) plan could be lower than the IRS-set levels.

On the other hand, many companies match workers' 401(k) contributions up to a certain percentage. Ideally, you should contribute enough to get your company's full match.

Roth 401(k)—Since 2006, a new type of defined contribution plan has been available: the Roth 401(k), or Roth 403(b), plan.

The Roth 401(k) contribution limits, both regular and catch-up amounts, are the same as for a regular 401(k). But this workplace retirement plan operates along the lines of the Roth IRA. Your Roth 401(k) deductions are made after taxes are taken out, so you don't get that immediate tax savings, but your eventual withdrawals from the account are tax-free.

Which is better? That depends.

A Roth 401(k) would be a better choice if you think your tax bracket in retirement will be the same or higher than it is now. A regular 401(k) has the edge if you think you'll end up in a lower bracket once you stop punching the time clock.

Getting to your money—Every cent you contribute to a 401(k) is yours from the minute it goes into the account. However, you have to wait a bit before any company match belongs fully to you. This process is known as vesting.

> Roth 401(k) deductions are made after taxes are taken out, so you don't get that immediate tax savings, but your eventual withdrawals from the account are tax-free.

Your employer sets up the vesting schedule. Generally, the vesting percentage increases every year you work for the employer until you own 100 percent of your company's matching amounts. It could take you up to seven years to fully vest if your company's plan was in place before 2006. However, a new tax law enacted that year now requires that newer plans allow workers to fully vest in a maximum six years. Remember, just because the law says a business has that long, a company could decide to offer a shorter vesting period.

You can take all of your vested account money with you if you change jobs.

You can take all of your vested account money with you if you change jobs. You can either roll the money into an IRA, or into your new employer's 401(k) plan.

However, you generally cannot spend your 401(k) savings until you turn 59½. If you take the money before that age, you'll have to pay not only the taxes due on the amount, but also a 10 percent early distribution penalty. In some cases, you might be able to take a loan from your 401(k), but not all employers offer such an option. If you do take a 401(k) loan and don't repay the money, or change jobs before repaying it, that's considered an early withdrawal, requiring tax and penalty payments.

Choose your investment wisely—Although your employer sets up your 401(k) plan, businesses usually hire a firm to offer plan choices and administer and manage the specific accounts from which you can choose. In most cases, your plan option will be a mutual fund. There should be a wide-enough array of plan choices to account for the various risk levels of employees.

Your company also may enable you to select company stock as your 401(k) investment. Don't go overboard here. Remember Enron. You already are getting a paycheck from the firm. If something happened to the business, you could lose not only your day-to-day living income, but your retirement money.

TRUTH

41

Retirement saver's credit

If you contribute to a retirement savings account, either at work or on your own, you might be able to get a double tax break.

The Saver's Credit provides low- and moderate-income workers the opportunity to offset part of their contributions to an IRA, as well as money put into a company retirement plan.

Because this is a tax credit instead of a deduction, you get more bang for your tax break buck. A tax deduction reduces your income, meaning the tax bill you compute using that income amount should be smaller.

But a credit is claimed after you arrive at your tax bill. The credit amount reduces that tax bill dollar-for-dollar. If you owe $1,000 and are eligible for a $500 credit, your tax bill is halved.

The Saver's Credit, originally called the Retirement Saver's Credit, was created to help workers, particularly those who stretch their day-to-day budgets to put something aside for retirement, recoup some of those contributions.

The credit could be as much as $1,000 per eligible taxpayers, meaning that for a husband and wife filing jointly, each could possibly qualify for the maximum tax break.

Just what is that maximum? It depends. There is no fixed Saver's Credit amount. Instead, the Saver's Credit is based on your filing status, how much you contribute to a qualified retirement account, and how much you earn. Basically, the lower your adjusted gross income (AGI), the larger your credit.

> The Saver's Credit provides low- and moderate-income workers the opportunity to offset part of their contributions to various retirement plans.

Income and contribution limits—Although you can put up to $5,000 (or more) into an individual retirement account and many thousand more into a 401(k), only $2,000 of your contributions count in figuring your credit amount.

Your actual Saver's Credit is a percentage—either 10, 20, or 50 percent—of that $2,000. Which percentage you use to calculate your credit depends upon your adjusted gross income. Basically, the smaller your adjusted gross income (AGI), the larger your credit.

If you're in the lowest income range, for example, and contribute at $2,000 or more to a retirement plan, you can claim 50 percent of $2,000, or $1,000. If you're married and both you and your spouse contribute at least $2,000 to your respective accounts, you each can take the maximum allowable credit amount for your income range, effectively doubling the tax break.

Another benefit of the Saver's Credit is that it is an add-on to other tax advantages associated with your retirement plan contribution. For example, Joe makes $15,000 a year, which puts him in the lower AGI range for purposes of claiming the Saver's Credit.

His employer does not offer a retirement plan, so Joe is able to deduct the $2,000 he contributed to his traditional IRA. (You can read more about this deduction opportunity in Truth 13, "Deducting without itemizing.")

Thanks to the Saver's Credit, Joe also can claim 50 percent of that same IRA contribution.

Effectively, Joe's one retirement contribution amount has shaved $1,300 off his tax bill. His IRA deduction accounts for a $300 tax saving because he's in the 15 percent tax bracket ($2,000 × 15 percent = $300). Then Joe gets to subtract the full $1,000 Saver's Credit from his eventual tax bill.

As Joe's case illustrates, the maximum benefit of the Saver's Credit goes to lower-income workers. It's phased out as your AGI increases, and if you make more than the top amount in your income range, you can't claim the credit at all.

The income ranges are adjusted annually for inflation. Form 8880, which you must file along with Form 1040 or 1040A to claim the credit, will contain the tax year's eligible income ranges and details on how to compute your credit.

What contributions to count—Contributions you make to traditional and Roth IRAs, as well as to your workplace 401(k) plan, or similar 403(b) or 457 accounts or other IRS-qualified company plans, can be used to figure your Saver's Credit amount.

The amount, however, is the total contributions to all these retirement plans.

If you put $2,000 into a Roth IRA and another $2,000 into your 401(k), even though you've contributed to two eligible retirement accounts, you can claim just one Saver's Credit. And the amount you use to figure that credit amount is the maximum $2,000, not the $4,000 you put into all your retirement accounts.

Other requirements—There also are a few special rules that apply to the Saver's Credit:

- You must be at least 18 years old to claim it.

- If you are listed as a dependent on someone else's return, you cannot take the credit.

- If you are a student, you cannot take the credit.

Also note that the Saver's Credit is nonrefundable. Your credit amount can help reduce your tax bill, even zero it out, but if your credit amount is more than any tax you owe, you lose the

The Saver's Credit is nonrefundable.

advantage of that excess amount. You can't claim it to get a refund.

TRUTH

42

Retirement plan rollovers

Did you recently change jobs? You're not alone. Labor statistics show that the average American switches jobs 11 times before retiring. During such a mobile career, that average worker could have enrolled in a separate retirement plan at each workplace.

The good news about all those retirement accounts you might have set up at your various jobs is that they probably are portable. Most employers today offer workers 401(k) retirement plans that you, the employee, are primarily responsible for funding. But that also means that at least part and maybe all of the account is yours to take with you when you leave a job.

You must ensure, however, that you follow the tax rules when you take your retirement account with you. A mistake in the process could be costly, not only in an immediate tax hit, but also to the long-term value of your savings.

401(k) transfer options—When you change jobs, you can do one of four things with your 401(k).

First, you can do nothing. You can leave the money in your former employer's plan. If you like the investment option there and you are not sure what your new company offers, this is not a bad move, at least for the short term. You do, however, lose the ability to continue adding to the account. You also might not be able to change your investment mix because you're no longer employed at the company.

And if your 401(k) balance is small, your former employer can decide it doesn't want to bother with the administration of a low-balance account owned by a former employee. The company can cash out your plan and send you the proceeds. If this happens, you'll lose 20 percent of your plan money to tax withholding.

Second, you can roll the money into a new 401(k) you establish at your new workplace. Most companies allow such a transfer.

Your third option is to roll the money into an IRA, either a traditional account or a Roth IRA. The Roth option became available in 2008. Before then, the traditional IRA was the only option because both the 401(k) and IRA money contained tax-deferred contributions and earnings, meaning tax is due when the money is distributed. Once the money was in the traditional IRA, you then could convert it to Roth IRA by paying the applicable taxes. But now, the two-step process is gone; you can send your 401(k) funds to a Roth and simultaneously pay tax on the converted amounts.

Finally, you can cash out your 401(k). But if you are younger than 59½, then you'll owe taxes on the full account, as well as a 10 percent early distribution penalty.

Indirect versus direct rollover—In all 401(k) transfer instances, you can either physically take the money yourself and complete the process or have the transfer done directly from the 401(k) to the qualified account of your choice.

> In all 401(k) transfer instances, you can either physically take the money yourself and complete the process or have the transfer done directly from the 401(k) to the qualified account of your choice.

An indirect rollover, in which you personally withdraw your retirement money and deposit it in a new IRA account or your new employer's plan, might be appealing if, for example, you are between jobs and need the cash to make ends meet temporarily. In this case, your former employer gives you a check for your 401(k) balance, less the IRS-required 20 percent withholding. You then have 60 days to put the money into a new IRS-approved retirement savings plan.

However, there's a big catch in this process. When you put your 401(k) money into an IRA or another company plan, you must put in the old account's full amount. That means you'll have to come up with the 20 percent that was withheld.

If you complete the rollover by the 60-day deadline, you can get back the 20 percent that was withheld when you file your next tax return. If you don't complete the rollover within the 60 days, the IRS keeps your 20 percent as down payment on the rest of the tax you might owe for taking possession of your retirement account too soon.

A more tax-smart option is a direct rollover. With this method, you can avoid the possibility of losing your 20 percent withholding and forfeiting your 401(k)'s tax-deferred status by having the account funds directly transferred to your new employer's plan or IRA. To complete a company-to-company transfer, talk with the HR and payroll offices at both your former and new workplaces. If you're putting the money into an IRA, the financial institution where you set up the account will have the paperwork you need.

The 1099-R will note the full retirement account money distributed, any taxes that were withheld, and, most important, the amount of the transferred account that is taxable.

Reporting your rollover—When you change jobs and take your 401(k) with you, the IRS wants to know. Your former employer, or usually the financial firm that manages the company's 401(k) plans, will report the transfer to you and the IRS via Form 1099-R.

The 1099-R will note the full retirement account money distributed, any taxes that were withheld, and, most important, the amount of the transferred account that is taxable. When you complete a direct trustee-to-trustee transfer, the 1099 should show the taxable amount as zero. In this case, the 1099-R also will include an explanatory code indicating that the money was transferred to another qualified retirement plan.

If you handled the transfer yourself and deposited the money into another qualified account in time to preserve your 401(k) distribution's tax-deferred status, you'll need to include a statement with your return explaining what you did.

One other tax form note. When you receive any retirement distribution, you must file either Form 1040 or 1040A. Retirement account payouts cannot be reported on the shortest Form 1040EZ.

TRUTH

43

Taxable Social Security benefits

You've stopped working, but that doesn't dissuade the IRS.

The agency finally gets to collect on your tax-deferred retirement accounts, with distributions from traditional IRAs and 401(k) taxed at your ordinary income tax rate. That same rate applies to the bit of extra cash you pick up from a part-time job.

The earnings from your other investments get a bit of a break, with tax on at least some of that money assessed at the lower capital gains rate.

And then there's Social Security. A sizeable chunk of your paychecks went to this federal program. Now you're looking forward to finally collecting your benefits.

The IRS might be collecting on those payments, too.

The effect of other income—When the Social Security system was created back in the thirties, the benefits were tax-free. However, over the years, laws have been enacted that allow for collection of tax on at least some Social Security payments.

The Social Security Administration says that less than one-third of beneficiaries pay taxes on their benefits. But statistics don't matter much if you're one of the retirees facing a bill from Uncle Sam on half or more of your Social Security.

So, will you have to worry about the IRS getting a piece of your federal retirement benefits? Maybe.

If your only retirement income is from Social Security checks, then you won't owe any tax on those payments. But if you have substantial income in addition to your Social Security, a portion of your federal benefits might be taxed.

Essentially, the planning you did for your retirement, some of it with the assistance of the tax code, could pose a Social Security tax problem. You have to tally all your retirement income. This includes distributions from tax-deferred savings, interest and dividends on taxable accounts, any wages or self-employment income, and any other taxable amounts, such as alimony.

In addition, you also must include any tax-exempt interest. This final figure is your modified adjusted gross income, or MAGI.

You then add one-half of your Social Security benefits, which are detailed on the Form SSA-1099 you get from the Social Security Administration each January, to your MAGI. This will produce your combined income amount, which is now compared to the Social Security taxation thresholds.

> If your only retirement income is from Social Security checks, then you won't owe any tax on those payments.

Threshold income levels—If you are a single filer, and your combined income is between $25,000 and $34,000, you may have to pay income tax on 50 percent of your benefits. If your earnings are more than $34,000, up to 85 percent of your benefits may be taxable. These thresholds also apply to taxpayers who file as head of household or qualifying widow or widower.

If you are married and file a joint return, you and your spouse must add each spouse's income and Social Security benefits to determine the taxable portion of your benefits. Couples could face taxes on 50 percent of their Social Security benefits if their combined income is between $32,000 and $44,000. When it exceeds $44,000, up to 85 percent of the benefits could be taxed.

If you're married but file separate returns, your threshold amount depends on whether you lived with your spouse during the tax year. If you did not share a residence at all during the tax year, you use the single taxpayer threshold amounts.

If you file a separate return from your spouse but you lived together at any time during the tax year, then you are more likely to owe taxes on your Social Security benefits. In this case, the threshold amount is zero.

Unlike some other tax thresholds that affect tax break eligibility, the Social Security earnings amounts are not indexed for inflation.

Pay as you earn—U.S. taxes are collected under a pay-as-you-earn system. That means that the IRS wants its portion of your income throughout the year as you receive it. That applies to taxable Social Security benefits just as it does to any other income.

If you find that you owe taxes on your Social Security benefits, you should either make quarterly estimated tax payments to the IRS or have federal taxes withheld from your benefits.

If you find that you owe taxes on your Social Security benefits, you should either make quarterly estimated tax payments to the IRS or have federal taxes withheld from your benefits. Many Social Security recipients find withholding is easier than filing Form 1040-ES vouchers four times a year.

You can choose to have 7, 10, 15, or 25 percent of your monthly benefit amount withheld. Indicate your withholding amount preference on IRS Form W-4V and mail or deliver it in person to your local Social Security office.

You can download a W-4V from the IRS web site (www.IRS.gov) or call the IRS at 1-800-829-3676 or the Social Security Administration at 1-800-772-1213 to request that a form be mailed to you.

SSI is not taxable—Also note the difference between Supplemental Security Income (SSI) and Social Security benefits.

SSI is a federal government benefit program that provides payments to eligible persons who are blind, disabled, or age 65 or older and who have little or no other income. Although SSI benefits are administered by the Social Security Administration, SSI benefits are not funded by Federal Insurance Contributions Act (FICA) taxes.

Unlike Social Security benefits, SSI benefits are not based on the recipient's prior work history, and in most cases, SSI payments are not taxable.

44

Required minimum distributions

Uncle Sam provided you some tax breaks over the years to help you build your retirement savings, so you shouldn't be surprised that he also has a plan in place to get his cut of your nest egg.

By April 1 of the year after you turn 70½, the tax code requires, in most cases, that you begin taking distributions from your tax-deferred retirement accounts. The IRS even tells you exactly how much you must withdraw.

These annual amounts are known as required minimum distributions, or RMDs, and are calculated by dividing your retirement's account's prior year-end value by a life expectancy factor in one of three RMD tables created by the IRS. Your precise minimum distribution will change each year as your age increases and your account balance drops.

The IRS's primary goal is to have you take out money each year so that the Treasury finally gets the taxes that have been deferred for years. But in setting up the system, the IRS did give some consideration to your retirement needs. A few years ago, the agency adjusted its life expectancy tables so that even with RMDs coming out each year, there still should be enough in your account to provide you with money through the rest of your life.

By April 1 of the year after you turn 70½, the tax code requires, in most cases, that you begin taking distributions from your tax-deferred retirement accounts.

The Uniform Lifetime Table is the most commonly used RMD chart. The other two are distribution tables for retirement account beneficiaries and account owners with much younger spouses. All three tables can be found in IRS Publication 590.

Which accounts must be tapped?—You generally have to take RMDs from any retirement account to which you made tax-deferred contributions or which had tax-deferred earnings.

These include traditional IRAs that you opened or rolled over, employer-provided regular retirement plans such as 401(k) or 403(b) plans, and self-employed plans such as SEP-IRAs or Keogh accounts.

If you have more than one IRA, you must calculate separately the RMD for each account. However, you withdraw the total from just one IRA or a portion from each of your IRAs.

For example, you have three traditional IRA accounts. You are required to take $500 from the first, $700 from the second, and $1,300 from the third. You can withdraw those amounts from the respective IRAs, you can have $1,250 from just two of your IRAs, or you can have a distribution of the total $2,500 from just one account. This enables you to evaluate which accounts are earning what and decide how you want to deal with the various investments.

If you inherited an IRA, the RMD on that account must be figured separately and can only be taken from that account.

Also be sure to double-check your account records regarding any nondeductible contributions you made to your traditional IRA. This includes the Form 8606s you filed with your tax returns, as well as your IRA account statements.

You don't have to pay taxes on nondeductible contribution amounts because you did not get a tax break when you put the money into your account. However, the subsequent earnings did accrue tax deferred and taxes are due on them.

Workplace RMDs, too—If in addition to your IRA (or IRAs), you have a workplace plan, usually a 401(k) plan, you must calculate that RMD separately.

In some cases where you are still working, you may be able to postpone your RMDs from a workplace account until you actually retire. Check with your firm's HR office and, of course, your own tax advisor.

RMDs at your pace—You also can take the year's required minimum distribution in installments. The IRS doesn't care if the cash comes out of the account weekly, monthly, quarterly, or whatever schedule you prefer, just as long as you take it out and pay the due taxes.

The total distributions for the year should be at least as much as the minimum required amount. Note that phrase "at least." If you need additional money, you can always take more than your RMD.

Keep track of the calendar, too. You generally have until April 1 of the year following the calendar year you turn 70½ to take your first RMD. In subsequent years, however, the deadline is December 31.

No RMDs for Roths—Roth accounts, both IRA and 401(k) versions, are exempt from the minimum distribution requirement because you already paid the taxes on your contributions to these accounts. And the IRS can't touch the tax-free withdrawals you make according to your, not the tax collector's, schedule.

Steep price for ignoring RMDs—If you have other investments you are using in your retirement, you might be tempted to leave your tax-deferred retirement accounts alone. Don't.

If you don't take your RMD on the IRS time table, you'll face an excess accumulation tax. This is 50 percent of the distribution that you didn't take.

The IRS might waive the penalty if you can show that you missed your RMD because of "reasonable error." You also have to demonstrate that you're taking steps to meet your RMD obligation.

> Although you must take out a specified amount each year from certain retirement accounts, you don't have to spend that money.

If you do overlook your RMD, file Form 5329 and pay the penalty. If the IRS later decides to accept your explanation, you'll get a refund of the penalty.

Withdraw, but reinvest—Although you must take out a specified amount each year from certain retirement accounts, you don't have to spend that money. If you don't need the cash to live on, you can invest it elsewhere. Of course, remember that the money then will be earning more income upon which you will owe taxes. But depending upon the investment's return, this might be a worthwhile move.

TRUTH

45

Estate taxes, or leaving it to your heirs, not the IRS

You worked hard to build a good life. When you pass along your assets, you want to make sure that your family and friends get the benefit, not Uncle Sam.

The good news is that only large estates are affected by the federal estate tax. The data show that only a small percentage of taxpayers—2 percent by the IRS' most recent count—end up owing the estate tax.

The bad news is that your estate may be larger than you realize.

The best news is that the estate tax is eliminated in 2010. The worst news is that it returns, with even tougher guidelines, in 2011. Congress, however, is likely to modify the estate tax before then. Most lawmakers agree that some estate tax is good but should be targeted to the ultra-wealthy.

Until Capitol Hill takes estate tax action, here are the tax issues you must consider when a loved one passes away.

Accounting for your estate—Your estate is essentially everything you own when you die. Your home and any other real property count. So do financial accounts, from your basic checking account to investment funds and equities to retirement plans. Don't forget insurance, personal belongings such as your car and jewelry, and collectibles.

> The best news is that the estate tax is eliminated in 2010. The worst news is that it returns, with even tougher guidelines, in 2011.

The total value of all these items is your gross estate. Subtract any debts and other adjustments, and you've got your taxable estate. Depending upon how much that figure is, you could, as the name implies, owe federal estate taxes. These taxes are due before your property is distributed to your heirs.

Estate tax rates—In 2001, the law was changed to gradually phase out the estate tax, which had topped out back then at 55 percent. At the same time, the estates under a certain value were exempt from any estate tax.

The rates and exemption amounts now in place are as follows:

Year of Death	Estate Tax Exemption	Estate Tax Top Rate
2008	$2 million	45 percent
2009	$3.5 million	45 percent
2010	No estate tax	No estate tax
2011	$1 million	55 percent

Special transfer rules—One of the most popular components of the estate tax has remained the same: the marital deduction. Under this law, all property in your estate can pass to your surviving spouse without being subject to the estate tax.

Even better, those exemption amounts discussed earlier don't apply. Any size estate can be transferred to the surviving spouse, meaning there is no estate tax liability upon the death of the first spouse.

But here's the catch. The estate is not technically tax free. Rather, the tax is deferred. When the surviving spouse passes away, the Treasury then will get a part of the estate. However, in the meantime, the surviving spouse has time to implement tax strategies that can lower any tax that might be assessed to her estate.

Some transfers of property also escape estate taxation when they go to qualified charities.

And when nonspouses inherit property, the basis is the value of the assets at the time of your death. This stepped-up basis means, in most instances, that when your heirs eventually sell the asset, the tax bill won't be as large as it would have been if the property had retained your original basis for capital gains computation purposes.

When gift taxes occur—In most cases, gifts are not taxable, either to the giver or the recipient. So, if you have a large estate, couldn't you simply knock it down to the exemption level by giving away your assets to family and friends before you die? The IRS thought of that, too. That's why the gift tax is a component of the estate tax.

You're not seeing things. Yes, you did just read that gifts aren't taxable. But you also read "in most cases" at that start of that sentence.

Transfers of several thousand dollars per year (the amount is indexed annually for inflation) can be made without immediate tax consequences. You can give away as much as you want, as long as you do so during the tax year in the allowable increments to separate recipients.

For example, in 2008, you gave your son, daughter-in-law, and three grandchildren $12,000. You reduced your estate's value by $60,000. If you're married, then you and your spouse each can give the kids and grandkids the allowable amount. In subsequent years, you (and your husband or wife) can again give each family member the allowable annual gift allowance amount. And while this example used children as the recipients, you can give the allowable gift amount to anyone.

But if you continue this process long enough to eventually give more than $1 million, you'll run into the gift tax exclusion amount. The gift and estate taxes are unified, requiring that your estate be considered not only with reference to the value of the property you left, but also to the value of gifts you made during your lifetime. This is how the IRS keeps you from giving away everything beforehand to avoid any taxes.

You also have to aware of the generation skipping tax, or GST, which applies to transfers of property to someone more than a generation younger. And there are many ways to structure estates to reduce tax costs. If you have a large or growing estate, it's usually worth the money to hire an experienced estate tax attorney.

> The gift and estate taxes are unified, requiring that your estate be considered not only with reference to the value of the property you left, but also to the value of gifts you made during your lifetime.

State inheritance and estate taxes—Some states impose their own taxes upon a resident's death. Most state estate tax laws are based upon federal law, and as the federal estate tax has been phased out, so have the state assessments.

A few states, however, decoupled their estate tax from the federal levy and continue to collect the tax. Check with your state's department of revenue for details.

There is no federal inheritance tax, but some states do collect this separate levy. Again, check with your state tax officials for details in your jurisdiction.

TRUTH

46

The trouble with
tax protests

*"The taxpayer. That's someone who
works for the federal government but
doesn't have to take the civil service
examination."*

—Ronald Reagan, 40th U.S. president

183

Want to end up in a federal jail cell? Buy into a tax protest argument, and you'll probably get your wish.

It sometimes takes awhile, but the Internal Revenue Service usually gets the men and women who insist that the U.S. government has no legal right to collect income taxes from individuals.

Just ask Irwin Schiff, convicted multiple times for his antitax efforts that spanned four decades. Then there are Edward and Elaine A. Brown, the tax-protesting couple who holed up in their New Hampshire home for months before finally surrendering in October 2007 and beginning their prison terms on tax evasion charges.

You don't even have to be a died-in-the-wool tax protester to pay the price. Actor Wesley Snipes was convicted in February 2008 of misdemeanor charges of not filing tax returns on the advice, he argued, of hired tax counsel. During the trial, testimony revealed that Snipes' advisors, who faced separate tax evasion charges, had used a classic tax protester argument as the basis for their advice.

The IRS doesn't like the term *tax protester*. Instead, the agency refers to such antitax positions as frivolous arguments. Whatever you call them, the truth is that refusal to pay your taxes will get you in big, and costly, trouble.

Accelerating the prosecution pace—Years ago, tax protesters pointed to the lack of prosecution of some of high-profile antitax advocates as evidence that their arguments were valid. But that's changing.

The IRS, facing a "tax gap" of money owed but not paid and nudged by Congress to bring in more revenue, has been more aggressive in bringing charges against tax protesters. And it's been largely successful.

Although in some instances, defendants have escaped tougher convictions (notably, the Snipes case), no court has ever ruled that the Internal Revenue Code is invalid or that the Internal Revenue Service has no authority to collect taxes.

In conjunction with legal action, the IRS also has made a concerted effort to educate taxpayers about the fallacies of the tax protest movement.

Fighting frivolous tax arguments—Although tax protesters are united in their belief that the income tax system is not valid, the reasons for these beliefs are as varied as the many antitax groups. Among the arguments are the following:

No court has ever ruled that the Internal Revenue Code is invalid or that the Internal Revenue Service has no authority to collect taxes.

- Tax filing violates freedom of speech protections.

- Only federal employees, or residents of territories and federal enclaves, such as Washington, DC, owe taxes.

- Income taxes are dependent upon a contractual arrangement between an individual and the government.

- The Internal Revenue Service is not a legitimate government agency.

Here's a closer look at three of the more popular tax protest arguments and the IRS's rebuttals.

The 16th Amendment was not properly ratified—The most popular antitax argument is that the IRS has no legal authority to collect income taxes because the 16th Amendment, which authorized the current income tax system, was not properly ratified.

However, the courts, including the Supreme Court, have consistently held that the Amendment, ratified on February 3, 1913, does properly allow collection of the income tax. It was ratified by 40 states. Subsequently, two other states also ratified the 16th Amendment, giving the measure more than the necessary three-fourths approval.

Tax filing is voluntary—Another persistent contention is that the filing of a tax return is voluntary. Proponents point to the fact that the IRS tells taxpayers in the Form 1040 instruction book that the tax system is voluntary. They also point to a 1960 Supreme Court opinion (Flora v. United States) which states, in part, that "[o]ur system of taxation is based upon voluntary assessment and payment, not upon distraint."

But in reality, the word "voluntary," as used in the Flora case and in IRS publications, refers to the system of allowing taxpayers to initially determine the correct amount of tax and complete the appropriate returns, rather than having the government determine tax for them from the outset. The requirement to file an income tax return is not voluntary, and that is specifically stated in the tax code.

Wages and other compensation are not income—This argument asserts that wages, tips, and other compensation an individual receives for personal services are not income. There are several variations of the argument. One is that the 16th Amendment authorizes a tax only on gain or profit. Wages don't meet this standard, argue tax protesters, because workers have basis in their labor equal to the fair market value of the wages they receive, meaning there is no gain to be taxed. A variation of this argument contends that wages are not taxable because Section 61 of the tax code does not specifically list wages as taxable income.

However, notes the IRS, "gross income" as cited in the Internal Revenue Code means all income from whatever source, including compensation for services—that is, wages. The only earnings that are not taxable are amounts that are, by tax law, specifically exempted or excluded. Courts have repeatedly upheld the IRS interpretation.

These three arguments and the IRS responses are part of a comprehensive collection contained in the document "The Truth About Frivolous Tax Arguments." You can download it at the IRS web site, www.IRS.gov.

TRUTH

47

Payment options

It used to be that the only way to pay your taxes was to write Uncle Sam a check. Times have definitely changed.

The IRS, or more specifically the U.S. Treasury, will still take your paper check. But there also are several other ways to pay any tax you owe.

Mailing it in—The old-fashioned payment check is still the favorite payment method for many taxpayers. One of its appeals is that you can write the check, which the tax agency says should be payable to the U.S. Treasury, not the Internal Revenue Service or IRS, as late as April 15, and then stick it in the envelope with your return that you mail at the last minute.

If this is your filing M.O., make sure you put enough postage on the return. If your tax package comes back to you because of insufficient postage, then your return and payment are late, and you'll face penalties and interest for missing the deadline. In fact, if you're using the U.S. Postal Service, send your return and payment via certified mail so that you'll have proof that you did file, and pay, on time.

Similarly, don't try that old trick of not signing your check. Like other creditors, the IRS won't buy that as an excuse, and you'll be nicked for late charges. Also be sure your check will clear. If your check bounces, the IRS may impose a penalty.

Plastic payments—Nowadays, millions of taxpayers pay their taxes the same way they pay for most other things: They charge it.

The IRS doesn't directly take your credit card. Rather, the agency has authorized two private companies to handle transactions. Both Link2Gov Corporation and Official Payments Corporation will accept your American Express, MasterCard, Visa, or Discover card.

> Nowadays, millions of taxpayers pay their taxes the same way they pay for most other things: They charge it.

You can pay online or by phone, as follows:

- Link2Gov Corporation
  www.pay1040.com
  888-PAY-1040 (888-729-1040)

- Official Payments Corporation
  www.officialpayments.com
  800-2PAY-TAX (800-272-9829)

There are many advantages to paying your taxes with plastic. It's easy. You can use this payment method if you mail in a paper return, or you can charge your tax bill when you electronically file your return. The charge amount can help you earn reward points.

However, paying the IRS by credit card has a few drawbacks. Both card processing companies charge a processing fee, usually around 2.5 percent of your tax bill. And after the amount is posted to your card account, you face the possibility of accruing interest charges.

Electronic payments—The IRS is a major proponent of electronic transactions, for both filing and paying your taxes. It's set up a couple of ways for you to e-pay your taxes.

With Electronic Funds Withdrawal (EFW), the IRS takes the money directly from your designated bank account to pay your tax bill. EFW payment is available through most tax preparation software and tax professionals. There is no charge by the IRS for this type of payment, but check with your bank about any fees it may charge.

Also known as direct debit or automatic payment, this system is essentially the same one used by many people to pay their other bills. Some folks, however, are not comfortable with the IRS having any semblance of access to their personal bank accounts.

Another electronic payment option is the IRS's Electronic Federal Tax Payment System (EFTPS). Here you set up an account at the EFTPS web site, https://www.eftps.gov/eftps/ and then sign on to make your payments, which are transferred from your bank account to the IRS. Any individual taxpayer can make EFTPS payments associated with Forms 1040 (for example, annual filing, estimated payments), 706 estate forms, 709 forms for gift taxes, or installment payments.

However, the system requires some lead time. Although you sign up for an EFTPS account online, you have to wait for a personal identification number, or PIN, to be mailed to you before you can use the online payment option. This could take up to 15 business days. So, if you're interested in EFTPS, plan ahead.

Installment payments—If you cannot pay your full tax bill, the IRS offers several installment plan options.

The advantage here is that you don't have to come up with a lump sum payment. Among the disadvantages is that you'll end up owing more than your tax bill. The IRS charges a one-time installment agreement fee of $105; if you make your installment payments by direct debit or have a low income, the fee is reduced.

You'll also be charged interest on the unpaid balance. And in most cases, the full bill must be paid within three years.

Details on installment agreement options can be found on Form 9465 and its instructions. The IRS also has an Online Payment Agreement application on its web site, www.IRS.gov.

Make an offer—If your tax bill is so large that you cannot pay it even in installments, consider making the IRS an offer. Under the Offer in Compromise (OIC) program, you propose an amount you can pay.

> The IRS recognizes that it's better sometimes to get some money sooner than spend years on collection efforts that still will not net the full amount due.

This is not a way to eliminate your tax liability. Rather, the IRS recognizes that it's better sometimes to get some money sooner than spend years on collection efforts that still will not net the full amount due.

You must make a reasonable offer, and the IRS requires documentation of your financial situation. In addition to an OIC application fee, you also must make a partial payment of your proposed settlement offer.

There are three OIC possibilities, as follows:

1. Lump-sum cash offer, payable in five or fewer installments.

2. Short-term periodic payment offer, where the offer amount must be paid within 24 months.

3. Deferred periodic payment offer, which calls for installments to be made for as long as the IRS legally can collect on the due tax.

A search of Offer in Compromise at www.IRS.gov will provide you with details on the various offer options, as well as the factors involved in making the IRS a payment proposal.

TRUTH

48

Tax penalties

The IRS relies on taxpayers to fill out their tax returns, correctly figure their tax bills, and then send both in by the filing deadline. But just in case, the IRS has the ability to assess penalties when tax forms and payments aren't properly made.

And that's just the tip of the penalty iceberg.

You could face a penalty for substantially understating your tax, filing an incorrect claim for a refund or credit, misstating a taxable transaction, or submitting a frivolous tax return.

If you provide fraudulent information on your return, expect the IRS to up the ante. In addition to a civil fraud penalty, you could face criminal prosecution.

The most common penalties are for filing late or paying taxes late. These are assessed separately, but when both apply, there are special rules as to the amounts that can be collected.

Late filing penalty—If you do not file your return by the due date, in April or later if you get an extension to file, you may have to pay a failure-to-file penalty. This is usually 5 percent of any tax due for each month or part of a month that your return is late. The maximum assessment is 25 percent of your unpaid tax amount.

> The most common penalties are for filing late or paying taxes late.

If you file your return more than 60 days after the due date, the minimum penalty is $100 or, if less, 100 percent of the tax on your return.

Late payment penalty—Next comes the penalty for not paying your tax bill on time. You will have to pay a failure-to-pay penalty of ½ of 1 percent (0.5 percent) of your unpaid taxes for each month, or part of a month, that the tax is not paid.

If you received an automatic six-month extension of time to file, this penalty doesn't apply to amounts unpaid as long as when you filed your extension request you paid at least 90 percent of your actual tax liability.

If you filed your return on time but weren't able to pay your tax bill and got an installment plan, you still face a failure-to-pay penalty.

However, the rate in this case is reduced to ¼ of 1 percent (0.25 percent) per month during any month in which the installment agreement is in effect.

But if the IRS has been sending you notices and you ignored them to the point that the agency is about to levy your assets, then the 0.5 percent rate increases to 1 percent of your unpaid tax.

Combined penalty—When both the late-filing and late-payment penalties apply, you actually get a bit of a break. The penalty for filing late is reduced by the penalty for paying late. That means the 5 percent late-filing assessment drops to 4.5 percent. The combined penalty then totals 5 percent (4.5 percent late filing plus the 0.5 percent late payment charge) of any of your unpaid tax.

Estimated tax penalties—Our tax system is based on a pay-as-you-earn approach. For employees, this is accomplished via payroll withholding. But when you have income that is not subject to withholding, such as self-employment income or investment earnings, you may have to make estimated tax payments during the year.

If you do not pay enough of your eventual tax liability through estimated tax payments, or withholding if you or your spouse with whom you file a joint return also has a job where payroll taxes are withheld, you may face an underpayment penalty.

Even when you do file the appropriate four estimated tax payments and end up with a refund, if you did not pay enough in each payment period to account for the earnings in that segment of the year, you may be charged a penalty.

Accuracy-related penalties—The IRS also is authorized to assess penalties when you substantially understate the amount of tax you owe on your return, as well as for "carelessly, recklessly or intentionally disregarding IRS rules and regulations."

This second instance is characterized by taking a position on your return that results in understated tax without trying to determine whether the position is correct. Knowingly taking a wrong tax stance, such as a credit for which you are not eligible, also falls into this category.

In both these penalty situations, the assessment is calculated as a flat 20 percent of the understated tax.

Negligence or ignorance of the law does not constitute fraud.

Civil fraud penalty—If you make fraudulent claims that produce a tax liability that is too low, the IRS can assess a penalty of 75 percent of the amount that was not paid due to that fraud.

Negligence or ignorance of the law does not constitute fraud. But when the IRS does find an intentional effort to deceive the agency, the case is referred to the IRS Criminal Investigation Division for possible criminal prosecution.

Keep in mind that both civil sanctions and criminal charges may be imposed.

Frivolous tax return penalty—If you file what the IRS deems a frivolous tax return, one that relies on false arguments about the legality of not paying taxes or filing returns, expect to be assessed a $5,000 penalty. If you jointly file a frivolous tax return with your spouse, both you and your spouse each may have to pay $5,000.

Penalty for bounced checks—If you write a check to the IRS and it bounces, you could face a penalty of 2 percent of the amount of the check. When the bounced check is $1,250 or less, the penalty is the amount of the check or $25, whichever is less.

Penalty relief—If you find yourself in a tax penalty situation, you might be able to convince the IRS that you shouldn't face the fees.

Through a process known as abatement, file Form 843 and provide the IRS with a good reason as to why the penalty should be reduced or dropped. Some common penalty reduction or abatement reason include serious illness; death of an immediate family member; and loss of your tax and financial records in a disaster or similar situation.

As in every tax situation, the more documentation you have, the better your chances to come out with a more favorable tax result.

TRUTH

49

Minimizing audit risks

"Income tax has made more liars out of the American people than golf.

—Will Rogers, humorist

Statistically, your risk of being audited is small. In 2007, for example, 1.4 million returns got a closer look from the IRS. But more than 140 million returns were filed that year.

The raw numbers don't matter, though, if your return ended up in that 1 percent.

So you don't have to spend time, and money, in connection with an audit, here are some ways to minimize IRS interest in your return.

Know audit triggers—It's no secret that certain tax moves get more attention from the IRS than others. These include excessive itemized deductions or claiming one of the popular business-related write-offs (home office, business use of a car, meals, and entertainment expenses). Familiarize yourself with the common audit red flags so that you can look at your return from an auditor's perspective.

Don't let fear of IRS scrutiny stop you from claiming any tax breaks to which you are legitimately entitled. Just be ready to show that everything on your return is correct if an auditor asks.

Uncomplicate your tax life—You don't want to draw any more attention to your return than necessary. Of course, your financial and tax situation determine in large part the complexity of your filing. But where you can, restructure your tax circumstances in ways that the IRS finds more benign.

> Don't let fear of IRS scrutiny stop you from claiming any tax breaks to which you are legitimately entitled.

For example, if you're self-employed and a lot of your clients pay you in cash, even when you report all the income, the IRS tends to suspect that some of those dollars are slipping through its grasp. Instead, ask your customers to pay you by check or electronically transfer the money to your account so that you'll have a more IRS-acceptable record. The IRS loves records, and if you show you have that same mindset, it's less suspicious.

Document, document, document—The best way to stop an auditor in his or her nitpicking tracks is to present thorough documentation for every claim on your return. (Are you seeing a pattern here?)

Make sure your tax records and corroborating documents are complete and easily accessible.

Make sure your tax records and corroborating documents are complete and easily accessible. In fact, attach copies of the relevant documentation to your tax return copy so that it is at your fingertips if the IRS asks for clarification. A good rule of thumb is if you don't have the necessary records, don't claim the expense.

Avoid round numbers—True, the IRS lets you round up or down the cents on your return entries. Your salary of $53,238.91, for example, becomes $53,239.00.

But when it comes to deductions, it's better to be precise. Don't estimate the value of the clothing you gave to Goodwill as $300 or your office supplies cost as $150. Be as specific as possible. Check those tax verification documents you've carefully kept and use the numbers shown on those receipts.

The argument against over estimation is that round numbers don't show up that often in real life. When a tax examiner sees a lot of them on a return, the natural inclination is to believe the figures were fabricated. And that could cause the IRS agent to wonder what else might be not-quite-right on your Form 1040.

Avoid questionable tax schemes—This seems obvious, but many taxpayers think they can slip something past the IRS. Don't try it. The IRS has become more aggressive in tracking down tax schemes, along with the promoters who sell them and the taxpayers who use them. This includes blatant tax-avoidance efforts, as well as more subtle tax-reduction moves that sound plausible.

If you have any questions about whether a tax break is allowable, you can be sure the IRS will feel the same way. Check with a reputable tax professional or call the IRS directly to ask about any tax claim about which you have concerns.

Don't put off the task—Few folks enjoy filing taxes, even when the process results in a refund. But if you wait until the last minute, your rush to finish could cause you to make costly mistakes.

And don't fall for the myth that filing at the deadline will protect you from audit because the IRS will be swamped with other procrastinators' returns, too. The timing of your filing has nothing to do with audit potential. All returns are eventually examined in the same manner.

Give yourself enough time to complete your return properly so that when the IRS looks at it, there aren't any mistakes that raise questions.

Use tax software—You might be more apt to file earlier if you use tax software. Another good thing about these programs is that they do the math for you, eliminating the addition and subtraction mistakes that often make the IRS pay extra attention to returns.

When you have your tax data on your computer, consider electronically filing. Not only will it help get your return through the system sooner, it means that one less IRS employee has to look at your form. Plus, when you send in a paper form, a person at the IRS Service Center must enter the numbers into the agency's computer system. Those transcribers are human; mistakes are sometimes made when your handwritten tax information is moved from your paper form to the IRS computers.

Double-check everything—Thoroughly double-check your return before submitting it, either by mail or electronically. If you've given yourself plenty of time to file, wait a day or two before doing your reassessment. Rested eyes tend to catch mistakes more easily.

A good test is to compare your current return to last year's version. If your life hasn't changed much, this will help ensure you don't overlook something.

If you're married, make sure your spouse looks over the 1040, too. Not only will that keep your wife or husband in the tax loop, but also he or she might see something that totally escaped your tax-weary eyes.

TRUTH

50

Preparing for an audit

The IRS wants to see you to talk about your tax return. Don't panic.

It might not be as bad as you think. Even if it is, you have no choice but to answer the tax examiner's questions.

But you can be prepared.

Know your audit type—You first want to clarify the type of return examination. The IRS conducts three basic inquiries, ranging from relatively routine, just-by-mail requests for information to more detailed, face-to-face audits.

If you must answer IRS questions, you want to do so via a correspondence audit. As its name indicates, you usually can provide the IRS what it wants by mailing the answers and documents. Most IRS audits are this relatively simple type.

Next comes the office audit. Here you're asked to report to your local IRS office to answer questions about your return. Although the meeting is in person, it's not that involved.

The field audit is the infamous process that most taxpayers dread. It typically is used for business filers, but some individuals also face field audits, especially when their personal returns include business income.

> The IRS conducts three basic inquiries, ranging from relatively routine, just-by-mail requests for information to more detailed, face-to-face audits.

In this case, the IRS agent prefers to come to your home to go over your tax return. You can, however, request to meet in a neutral location, such as your accountant's office. The reason you want to keep the agent out of your house is that he or she might see things that prompt further inquiries. For example, the auditor doesn't know that the antique crystal in your display cabinet was a bequest from your grandmother. He might wonder how you can afford expensive collectibles on the salary shown on your return.

Get professional help—Even if your return is relatively simple and you're confident you can satisfy the auditor's questions, don't go into an audit alone. This probably is your first audit; the IRS agent has been through hundreds or more. Even if it's not adversarial, you want to be on as equal footing as possible.

Enrolled agents, tax attorneys, and CPAs are authorized to represent you at an audit. Hire one. These professionals are trained in tax law, know the arcane language of taxes, and have handled audits before. More importantly, the audit is not a personal affront to them; they aren't going to get emotional and say something that could make matters worse.

In fact, these tax pros know when it's best to say nothing at all. Almost every tax professional has a tale of the client who inadvertently told the IRS examiner something that made the original audit more of an ordeal.

Know your rights—Even if you hire a professional to help you through the audit, know your rights. IRS Publication 1 details the Taxpayers' Bill of Rights, including a section specifically discussing what to expect during an audit.

If you don't have professional counsel and the audit is not going well, you can ask for the process to stop so that you can get help.

If you believe the IRS agent is treating you unfairly or unprofessionally, you have the right to report it to the employee's supervisor. If the supervisor's response is not satisfactory, you can take it further up the chain of command.

Collect requested information—You can help your audit counsel by making sure you have all the data and documents related to your audit. After you've found the relevant material, organize it. You, or your representative, want to be able to immediately pull out the information the agent requests. Not only does that address the factual issue, but it also demonstrates that you take your tax filing seriously.

However, don't over-document. Only bring records that are related to the area of your return under question. If you have extraneous material, you could hand the examiner irrelevant material. Not only is that sloppy, but other receipts could raises additional questions.

Behave professionally—Just as the IRS agent is required to treat you appropriately, you should do the same. Show up for the meeting on time. Dress in a business-like manner.

Remember that the audit is not necessarily the final say on your return.

Be polite, but not overly sociable. The IRS examiner is not your friend; he or she is there to make sure you pay the appropriate amount of tax. You and your advisor are there to make sure you don't overpay your tax.

Similarly, don't argue with the agent. Make your case on the facts. If the auditor disagrees, express your objections, but let it go. Remember that the audit is not necessarily the final say on your return.

Appeal the results—You showed up, brought along a tax professional, argued your case, and the auditor still said pay up. What now?

The IRS will send you a report or letter that explains the proposed adjustments. Read it carefully. If you disagree with the findings, don't sign the letter and initiate an appeal. The letter outlines the steps and the time frame in which you must take them; don't miss the deadlines.

You can start by talking with an IRS Appeals officer. Although appeals conferences are informal meetings, come prepared with records and documentation to support your position. You also can bring your attorney or accountant to the meeting.

If you're not able to reach a satisfactory agreement within IRS internal channels, you can take your case to Tax Court. It might be more effective, though, to talk with the Taxpayer Advocate Office. Although it's part of the IRS, the Taxpayer Advocate is an independent organization created to help taxpayers, at no charge, resolve tax problems.

There's at least one local Taxpayer Advocate in every state. An interactive map (found by searching for Taxpayer Advocate at the IRS web page, www.IRS.gov) can help you find the nearest Taxpayer Advocate Office. You also can call 1-877-777-4778 to see if your situation qualifies you for the free assistance.

TRUTH

51

Taxpayers abroad and military filers

The U.S. tax system applies to income regardless of where in the world it is earned. That means Americans who are abroad, either for private-sector jobs or as members of the armed forces, still must pay taxes to Uncle Sam.

However, the IRS does recognize the special circumstances of these taxpayers and makes some allowances.

Employees abroad—U.S. citizens (or resident aliens) who live outside the United States are subject to the same general filing requirements as taxpayers within America's borders. That means the IRS wants its rightful part of the paycheck you bring home to your overseas abode.

But you may be able to limit the amount that returns to the U.S. Treasury by taking advantage of the foreign earned income exclusion. Each year, you are allowed to keep a portion of your foreign earnings off the U.S. tax rolls as long as you meet three conditions.

First, your tax home must be in the foreign country. For U.S. tax purposes, this is the general area of your main place of employment. Your family home might still be in Nebraska, but if you are working full-time for a company in Milan, Italy, then Milan is your tax home.

Second, you must have foreign earned income. The earned income definition is the same as within the United States, generally: wages, salary, or professional fees.

Finally, you must be a bona fide resident of the foreign country or demonstrate what the IRS calls a "physical presence" there.

You meet the bona fide resident rule if you live within the foreign country for an entire tax year. You can meet the physical presence test by living in the foreign nation for 330 days over 12 months. The 330 days do not have to be consecutive.

Essentially, the residency requirements are to ensure that you are indeed living and working in the country, not just globe-trotting and taking advantage of the foreign earned income exclusion.

The exclusion amount is adjusted annually for inflation. Check www.IRS.gov for the latest figure. It also applies to each filer, so an eligible husband and wife working abroad can each exclude the amount, doubling the foreign earnings amount that is free of U.S. taxes.

The exclusion helps offset the taxes you pay in the country in which you are working. But not every nation is treated as foreign for this tax exclusion purpose. If you live and work in U.S. possessions such as Puerto Rico, Guam, the Commonwealth of the Northern Mariana Islands, the U.S. Virgin Islands, or American Samoa, you won't be able to exclude those earnings from tax.

Foreign housing exclusion or deduction—In addition to the foreign earned income exclusion, you can also claim an exclusion or a deduction for your foreign housing costs. You must meet the same bona fide residence or physical presence tests to qualify for this tax benefit.

The amount of qualified housing expenses eligible for the housing exclusion or deduction is limited to a percentage of the year's foreign earned income exclusion amount. In response to concerns of taxpayers working and living in countries with high housing costs, the IRS has compiled a list of nations that qualify for added housing expense limits.

You can find details on those countries and the adjustment amounts, as well as how to file for these benefits, in IRS Publication 54, Tax Guide for U.S. Citizens and Resident Aliens Abroad. It's downloadable at www.IRS.gov.

Higher tax cost to expatriate—If you decide you want to make a foreign country your permanent home, you can relinquish your U.S. citizenship. However, you'll pay a tax price for expatriation. At the time you officially are no longer a U.S. citizen, any capital assets you own will be taxed, at current market rates, on their unrealized gains. If you're considering this move, discuss the implications with your tax adviser.

Combat pay considerations—
Members of the Armed Forces, active or on reserve, also must follow U.S. tax rules. However, special tax consideration is given to the circumstances faced by members of the military.

Combat pay is nontaxable. Given the circumstances under which it is

> Special tax consideration is given to the circumstances faced by members of the military.

earned, it is a welcome tax break. However, some service personnel receiving only or primarily nontaxable money found they were denied some other tax breaks.

Now members of the military can choose to count that money as income when it comes to figuring eligibility for the Earned Income Tax Credit (EITC). The EITC is a tax break created for lower-income workers. Similarly, members of the armed forces can count combat pay as earned income for IRA contribution purposes.

As for taxpayers stationed in combat zones, the IRS typically suspends compliance actions, such as audits or collections, until the service member has been returned from the hazard area for 180 days.

As for taxpayers stationed in combat zones, the IRS typically suspends compliance actions, such as audits or collections, until the service member has been returned from the hazard area for 180 days. If you or a family member qualifies for this relief, you can notify the IRS directly via a special e-mail address: combatzone@irs.gov.

Military home sale exclusion exception—Military men and women also found that they weren't always able to take advantage of the home-sale exclusion. Generally, when you live in your primary residence for two of the five years before you sell, you don't have to pay tax on profits up to $250,000 if you're a single taxpayer, or $500,000 if you're married and file a joint return.

Some service personnel, however, lost the full sale exemption because they were redeployed before meeting the two-year residency requirement. So, the tax law was changed to exempt affected military home sellers from the two-year rule. They now qualify for the full exclusion if they move early to meet service commitments.

More on military tax breaks and requirements can be found in IRS Publication 3, Armed Forces Tax Guide, downloadable at www.IRS.gov.

TRUTH

52

Tax help in disastrous times

When a natural catastrophe strikes, the Internal Revenue Service can provide some much-needed relief.

If the disaster hits around a filing deadline, the IRS is understanding. It usually allows you extra time to complete your paperwork.

And regardless of when in the year, or tax-filling cycle, you encounter an unexpected loss, you might be able to get back some tax money, possibly within weeks of the disaster, to help you make repairs.

What counts as a casualty—Because of the attention that major natural disasters receive, we tend to think that it is only in those extreme cases that federal aid is available. However, the tax code can come to the rescue when you experience a smaller, but no less devastating, casualty loss.

For tax purposes, a casualty loss can come from the damage, destruction, or loss of your property from any sudden, unexpected, and unusual event. This, of course, includes floods, hurricanes, tornadoes, ice storms, blizzards, wildfires, earthquakes, mudslides, and even drought if it hits an area suddenly.

But in addition to those natural disasters, the tax code considers as casualties such unwelcome events as burglaries and thefts, structure fires, and vandalism. In some instances, even damage from a car crash might be deductible as a casualty loss.

In each of these instances, you can claim a portion of your losses when you file your tax return.

What doesn't count as a casualty—The IRS realizes that some events might be unexpected, but the agency still won't allow you to claim just any damages as a casualty loss.

For example, accidental breakage of articles, such as glassware or china, under normal conditions doesn't count. Neither does property damage caused by a family pet.

One disallowed area that frustrates many taxpayers is what the IRS calls "progressive deterioration." An example of this is termite damage to your home. Although it might well be unexpected, the IRS says that since the damage results from a steadily progressing cause rather than one sudden event, it is not eligible to be claimed.

Other such disallowed damages include the steady weakening of a building due to normal wind and weather conditions or destruction of landscape plants by disease or pests. However, if the infestation is unexpected or unusual, that might qualify as a casualty loss.

Special timing for major disasters—When an area is designated a major disaster area by the president, which is the norm after Mother Nature gets nasty, special tax rules apply.

When an area is designated a major disaster area by the president, which is the norm after Mother Nature gets nasty, special tax rules apply.

The key consideration in these cases is that you can choose which tax year to claim your disaster losses. That timing factor might help get you more money, and get it sooner, from the IRS.

Generally, casualty losses are deductible in the year they occurred. For example, your home suffered fire damage in June 2008. You would claim any eligible losses on your 2008 return when you file it in 2009.

But if the loss is the result of a presidentially declared disaster, you can choose to deduct that loss on your tax return for the previous year.

If your home's June 2008 damage was the result of a tornado, and the president declared the region a major disaster, you could choose to claim the loss on your 2008 return or file an amended 2007 return using Form 1040X. Which filing would be more advantageous depends on your 2007 tax filing data and your expected 2008 filing situation.

In this case, let's assume you claimed the standard deduction on your 2007 return. Now you can amend that filing and claim a larger itemized amount because of the extensive tornado damage to your home. This revised filing will get you a refund and will do so relatively soon after the storm struck your property, providing you money to make repairs.

When you have the choice of which tax year to file, prepare a draft return for each. In doing so, if you find that it would be more advantageous, tax-wise and financially, to wait and claim the disaster losses on your upcoming return next year, then do that.

Other tax data you might need—Sometimes, your tax documents from prior years might be lost or damaged in the disaster. Because you will need that information if you decide to file an amended return, you need to contact the IRS to get copies.

By filing Form 4506, Request for Copy of Tax Return, you can request full copies of the previous four years of income tax returns. Write the appropriate disaster designation, such as "Hurricane Gustav," in red letters across the top of the form so that the IRS will expedite processing of your request and waive the normal user fee.

The IRS also maintains a special web page with news of disaster relief, related tax issues, and disaster-related publications, forms, and worksheets; type "disaster situations" in the search box at the top right of www.IRS.gov.

Epilogue

Did you find yourself in these pages? You and your family probably showed up in several chapters. Next year, the sections that applied to you are likely to change.

That's the ultimate truth about taxes: They are dynamic, not just because lawmakers in Washington, DC, insist on tweaking the Internal Revenue Code every year, but because of how our changing lives intersect those laws.

As your life progresses, remember that somewhere in those tens of thousands of tax laws are opportunities. So don't let taxes overwhelm you. Take advantage of them.

Stay informed. Keep up with the tax code changes that are inevitable.

Stay involved. Let your federal lawmakers know what you think about their proposed changes to tax laws.

And stay on top of your taxes. Don't think about them just in April, but year round, when you have a chance to put some of the provisions to use in a positive way in your life.

By doing so, you'll fulfill your responsibility, as Justice Oliver Wendell Holmes noted, to help fund our great American civilization and also reap the benefits that many of those tax laws afford.

Finally, a few "thank-you"s.

Thanks to my friends and colleagues who, although they hate taxes, continue to ask questions about them that keep me on my tax toes.

Thanks to Jim Boyd of Pearson for recognizing that taxes are indeed a worthy topic for a book, and his colleague Russ Hall for helping make sure it was understandable.

And thanks to my husband for his patience and encouragement in this and everything.

About the Author

S. Kay Bell has been writing about taxes for a decade, but following the subject—as a taxpayer, journalist, Congressional staff member, and government relations specialist—for most of her journalism career. After two decades in Washington, DC, including stints on Capitol Hill and with two major multinational corporations, she helped launch the tax channel at the popular personal finance website, Bankrate.com. She still writes for Bankrate, including the site's tax blog, *Eye on the IRS*.

In addition, Bell posts daily at her own personal finance blog, *Don't Mess with Taxes*, where *The Wall Street Journal* praised her ability to effectively put her personal finance advice in a social or historical context. Her writing also appears in numerous mass-circulation publications and websites, including USAToday.com, TheStreet.com, MarketWatch.com, and AOL.com, and she is regularly interviewed by media outlets ranging from National Public Radio's "Marketplace" to Yahoo's "Generation Debt."